A Taste of Florida

The Best of
"Thought You'd Never Ask"

A Taste of Florida

The Best of
"Thought You'd Never Ask"

By Dorothy Chapman
Edited By Heather J. McPherson

A publication of The Orlando Sentinel
Sentinel Books
Orlando/1990

Written by Dorothy Chapman
Edited by Heather J. McPherson
Designed by Eileen Schechner
Cover photos by Tom Burton
Printed in the United States by R.R. Donnelley

ISBN 0-941263-19-3

Chapman, Dorothy, 1921-
    A Taste of Florida : The Best of "Thought You'd Never Ask" /
By Dorothy Chapman ; edited by Heather J. McPherson — 1st ed.
        p. cm.
    "A publication of The Orlando Sentinel."
    Includes index.
    ISBN 0-941263-19-3 : $18.95
    1. Cookery. I. McPherson, Heather J. II. Title.
TX714.C464 1990
641.5 — dc20   90-21434
                                                              CIP

About the author

Dorothy Chapman is a retired food editor from *The Orlando Sentinel*. She was born in New York, grew up in Arizona and graduated from Arizona State University in Tempe.

Before moving to Orlando in 1959, Chapman was a writer and radio commentator, an advertising manager for a large Western retail store and had her own advertising and public relations business.

In Central Florida, she worked briefly at a weekly newspaper, the now-defunct Corner Cupboard. At *The Orlando Sentinel* she started as a society writer. Before she became the *Sentinel's* food editor in 1971, Chapman had been women's editor, Lake County editor and fashion editor.

In her early days as food editor, Chapman was a one-woman show — writing stories and headlines, laying out pages, editing wire-service stories. She learned as she went. She won awards both for writing and for layout (plaques fill a whole wall in the hallway of her south Orlando home). She served as president of both the Florida Press Club and the Central Florida chapter of the Society of Professional Journalists, Sigma Delta Chi. She also has testified about nutrition for a U.S. Senate subcommittee and is a former judge for the Pillsbury Bake-Off.

Her "Thought You'd Never Ask" column, which has run for more than 15 years, provides readers with their favorite restaurant recipes, cooking tips and suggestions on how to locate hard-to-find ingredients. However, the restaurant recipe requests always have been the backbone of the popular Food section feature.

Chapman retired from the *Sentinel* in 1986, but she continues to write "Thought You'd Never Ask" for the Food section. Retirement to Chapman has meant a full schedule of volunteer work (most notably with the annual Gourmet Gala, a benefit for the March of Dimes), free-lance writing for national publications and outings with family and friends.

Chapman has three daughters, Amy Elliot Lutz, who is co-owner of Elliot's Cafe in Winter Park, Fla.; Rosemary Chancellor ("the best cook of the family") of Windermere, Fla., who is a regional business manager for Sears, Roebuck and Co.; and Deborah Snyder of Hammond, Ind., who is business manager of a computer training school. Chapman has four grandchildren.

Acknowledgments

When it comes to cooking, many people think that too many cooks spoil the broth. Well, that may be so, but when it comes to putting together a cookbook you can never have enough help. *A Taste of Florida* would not have been possible without the support and guidance of the following:

Heather J. McPherson, food editor of *The Orlando Sentinel,* who edited this book.

Betty Boza and Phyllis Gray of the *The Orlando Sentinel* test kitchen staff and *Sentinel* food writer Charlotte Balcomb Lane who tested the recipes.

Art director Eileen Schechner and photographer Tom Burton who designed and photographed the cover photo.

Chef Jim Alexander of Sweets, Etcetera in Orlando for making the delicious Key Lime pie that graces the cover. (You'll find the recipe on page 196.)

Christian Dior for supplying the pie server, cake plate and dessert fork used in the cover photo.

And last, but not least, all of the talented Florida chefs who have provided *The Orlando Sentinel* readers with wonderful recipes in "Thought You'd Never Ask."

To my daughters
Amy, Rosemary and Debbie —
love, pride and dreams fulfilled.

Contents

Introduction

I thought you'd never ask, but thank you so much for doing so.

For more than 15 years, letters from *The Orlando Sentinel* Food section readers to my column, "Thought You'd Never Ask," have been delightful, funny, dear and sincere. Among the most gratifying letters are those requesting a very special recipe from a wonderful dining experience that occurred at a Florida restaurant. Helping someone re-create part of a memorable meal in their home kitchen is satisfying indeed.

Recipes included in this collection were provided by the restaurants and have been compiled from more than a decade of "Thought You'd Never Ask" columns.

Some of the recipes are from restaurants that are under new management, others may be no longer on the menu and a few are treasured gems from restaurants that are no longer in existence. However, all are an important part of Florida's culinary history.

These recipes have been tested over the years in professional kitchens throughout the state. Now enjoy them in your home. They are on the house, compliments of the chef.

Dorothy Chapman

Appetizers

The secret to this appetizer's success is in the preparation. Chef Bruno Wehren's recipe calls for deep-frying the vegetables separately to avoid overcooking.

Outback Restaurant's Fried Onion and Potato Strips
Buena Vista Palace, Lake Buena Vista

1¼ **pounds white onions,**
  peeled
1¼ **pounds baking potatoes,**
  peeled
All-purpose flour for dusting
Salt and pepper to taste
1 quart vegetable oil

Cut onions in half and slice into thin strips; set aside. Using a grater, cut potatoes lengthwise, creating long, thin strips; set aside.

Add salt and pepper to flour to taste.

In a deep-fryer, heat vegetable oil to 350 F.

Flour onions, coating each strip well. Shake off excess flour. Deep-fry onions in hot oil until golden brown. Remove onions from fryer and drain off excess oil.

Coat and deep-fry potatoes following the same procedure. Toss onion and potato strips together and serve hot.

Makes 6 servings.

The Outback
RESTAURANT

For a variation, add finely chopped bacon, onions, pepperoni or green pepper to this stuffing mixture.

Le Cordon Bleu's Mushroom Caps With Crab Meat Stuffing
Winter Park

24 jumbo mushrooms
¼ stick butter
3 tablespoons flour
1 cup milk
1 cup grated Gruyere cheese
1 pound Alaskan snow crab,
    cut in small pieces
2 eggs
1 tablespoon fresh chopped
    parsley
3 cloves garlic, finely minced
    or crushed in a garlic press
1 tablespoon fresh chives
Salt and pepper to taste
Nutmeg to taste
Butter seasoned with garlic
    to taste

Preheat oven to 400 F.

Remove stems from mushrooms and boil caps for 2 minutes in water. Drain.

Melt ¼ stick of butter and stir in flour to make a roux. In another pan, bring milk to boil; slowly pour hot milk into roux, whisking until smooth. Remove from heat. Allow mixture to cool.

Combine cheese, crab and seasonings with eggs and mix well. Stir cheese mixture into roux. Spoon stuffing into mushroom caps.

Dot caps with garlic butter and bake for 5 minutes or until slightly browned.

Makes 4 servings.

Vinton's New Orleans Restaurant in Lake Wales has offered Floridians a taste of Louisiana cooking for more than a decade. These sweet fritters are a perfect appetizer for holiday menus.

Vinton's New Orleans Restaurant's Pumpkin Fritters
Lake Wales

1 cup all-purpose flour
$\frac{1}{2}$ cup sugar
1 teaspoon freshly grated
   nutmeg
Dash ground cloves
Ground ginger to taste
$\frac{1}{8}$ teaspoon cinnamon
$\frac{1}{2}$ teaspoon baking powder
1 cup water
1 pound can solid-pack
   pumpkin
2 cups vegetable oil
Confectioners' sugar for
   dusting

Combine flour, sugar, nutmeg, cloves, ginger, cinnamon and baking powder in a large bowl. Make a well in the center of the dry ingredients and fill well with 1 cup of water. Gradually drain the flour mixture from the inner edge of the well into the center, stirring to incorporate ingredients. Continue procedure until water and dry ingredients are well-blended. Add pumpkin and mix thoroughly. Let batter stand at room temperature for 30 minutes.

Heat oil in a deep-fryer or a large, heavy skillet to 375 F. Drop batter into oil by teaspoonfuls (do not crowd) and fry until brown, turning frequently, about 5 minutes. Drain on paper towels. Dust with confectioners' sugar and serve immediately.

Makes 8 servings.

VINTON'S
New Orleans
RESTAURANT & LOUNGE

This popular Mexican dish can be used as a dip for crisp tortilla chips, a light sauce for grilled seafood or a topping for tacos and burritos.

Casa Gallardo's Perfect Guacamole
Locations throughout Florida

2 tablespoons minced onion
1 medium jalapeno
1 garlic clove, minced (optional)
2 teaspoons fresh coriander (do not substitute ground coriander)
Juice of $^1/_2$ lime
2 large ripe avocados, pitted and peeled
1 large tomato, peeled, seeded and chopped
Salt and extra lime juice to taste
Tortilla chips

Combine $1^1/_2$ tablespoons onion with jalapeno, garlic, coriander and juice of $^1/_2$ lime in the work bowl of a food processor or blender. Chop ingredients using the pulse button or the on-off switch until mixture is almost pureed. Put mixture into a mixing bowl.

Mash avocado into jalapeno and onion mixture with a fork. Add chopped tomato and remaining minced onion to avocado mixture. Stir to blend. Season with salt and additional lime juice.

Serve chilled or at room temperature with tortilla chips.

Makes 4 to 6 servings.

Test kitchen note: This dip can be prepared several hours ahead and stored in the refrigerator until ready to serve. Lime juice sprinkled over the guacamole will prevent the mixture from darkening.

Restaurant owner Chris Christini serves this eggplant mixture, instead of butter, as a spread for crusty Italian bread. It makes a terrific dip for fresh vegetables, too.

Melanzana a la Christini
Christini's Ristorante Italiano, Orlando

2 medium eggplants
¼ bunch fresh dill
Juice of ½ lemon
1 tablespoon olive oil
1 pint mayonnaise
¼ tablespoon salt
¼ tablespoon white pepper
2 tablespoons fresh garlic that
   has been minced or crushed
   in a garlic press

Preheat oven to 375 F.

Pierce eggplants with fork.

Put eggplants on a baking sheet and place in preheated oven. Bake for 1 hour or until tender. When the eggplants are cool enough to handle, cut them in half and remove the peel. Cube remaining eggplant meat.

Place eggplant cubes and remainder of ingredients in a blender or food processor container and process until smooth.

Makes about 6 to 8 cups.

Rich, buttery pine nuts and flavorful spinach combine to make this wonderful dip. Serve it with fresh vegetables or crisp, cheese-flavored bread sticks.

Edibles Etcetera's Spinach Pine Nut Dip
Altamonte Springs

2 packages frozen chopped
  spinach, uncooked
2¹/₂ cups mayonnaise
1¹/₂ cups sour cream
2 tablespoons Worcestershire
  sauce
Dash Tabasco sauce
¹/₂ cup grated onion
¹/₄ cup chopped scallions
¹/₂ cup plus 1 tablespoon pine
  nuts, toasted
¹/₂ cup chopped parsley
1¹/₂ teaspoons salt
³/₄ teaspoon pepper
1 head red cabbage, hollowed

Thaw and squeeze all liquid from spinach. Mix all ingredients except 1 tablespoon of pine nuts. Cover mixture and refrigerate. When ready to serve, put dip in hollowed red cabbage. Garnish with remaining tablespoon of toasted pine nuts.

Serve this garlic mixture with potato chips, bell pepper strips, crunchy carrot and celery spears or fresh button mushrooms.

Edibles Etcetera's Garlic Dip
Altamonte Springs

1 head fresh garlic
2 (8-ounce) packages
  Neufchatel cheese
¹/₂ cup mayonnaise
2 tablespoons dried green
  onion flakes

Remove paper skin from garlic head and separate cloves. Crush cloves in a garlic press.
  Soften Neufchatel cheese.
  Mix all ingredients together. Cover and refrigerate until ready to serve.

These crisp, deep-fried pickles, which were created by chef Rene Weibel, can be sliced and served as tangy nibbles on a party tray. Kosher pickles can be substituted for plain dill.

Grand Floridian Beach Resort's Fried Pickles
Lake Buena Vista

½ cup flour
1 cup cornmeal
¼ teaspoon baking powder
1 bunch cleaned and trimmed
  scallions, chopped finely
3 whole eggs
¼ cup milk
¼ teaspoon salt
1 teaspoon sugar
¼ teaspoon cayenne pepper
About 20 dill pickles,
  depending on size
Vegetable oil for deep-frying

Heat vegetable oil in a deep-fryer.

Slice pickles lengthwise into quarters; set aside. Mix together the balance of ingredients. If batter is too thick, slowly add more milk. Dip pickles in batter to coat.

Deep-fry the battered pickles in hot vegetable oil until they are golden brown.

Remove the pickles with tongs and drain on paper towels. Serve hot.

Makes 20 deep-fried pickles.

This warm dip is best served with unsalted crackers, slices of fresh Cuban bread or jicama strips.

Classic Creations Catering's Warm Artichoke Dip
Winter Park

1 (14-ounce) can artichoke
   hearts (not marinated)
1 cup low-calorie mayonnaise
1 package dry Good Seasons
   Italian Dressing mix
1 cup grated Parmesan cheese

Drain artichoke hearts and squeeze until excess liquid is removed. Place in food processor bowl and, using the on-off switch or the pulse button, chop into small, coarse pieces. Be careful not to puree the artichokes.

Put chopped artichokes into a mixing bowl and blend in balance of ingredients. Mix well.

Spoon artichoke mixture into microwave-safe serving dish, cover and vent with plastic wrap. Microwave on high (100 percent) power for 2 to 3 minutes, stirring at least every minute.

The mixture should not be overcooked, just well-heated and blended.

Serve immediately with Melba toast or crackers of choice.

Makes 10 servings.

This recipe can perform double-duty in the kitchen. Serve as a dip with assorted vegetables or coat chicken breasts with mixture before baking.

Meiner's Catering's Curried Chutney Dip
Orlando

2 cups Major Grey's chutney
1 tablespoon curry powder
Ground ginger to taste
1 teaspoon confectioners'
  sugar
Juice and grated rind of
  ½ lemon
1 garlic clove, minced
1 quart mayonnaise
2 cups sour cream

Combine chutney, curry, ginger, sugar, lemon juice, grated rind and garlic. When thoroughly mixed, stir in mayonnaise and sour cream. Adjust seasonings to taste.
  Makes 2 quarts.

This pesto sauce can be served over any type of pasta or used as a dipping sauce for tortellini.

Garden Terrace's Pesto Sauce
Marriott's Orlando World Center, Orlando

1¹/₂ cups chopped fresh basil
  leaves
2¹/₂ tablespoons dried oregano
1¹/₄ cups plus 2 tablespoons
  olive oil
1 pound pine nuts
Salt and black pepper to taste

Combine all ingredients in a blender at high speed for 4 to 5 minutes. Every 40 to 50 seconds wipe down the inside of the blender container with a rubber spatula to make sure the ingredients are completely mixed.

The sauce should be covered and stored in the refrigerator until ready to serve.

Makes enough sauce for 10 servings.

This liver pate can be served with unsalted crackers, French bread slices or an assortment of cheeses.

Crackers Oyster Bar's Pate
Church Street Station, Orlando

1 pound chicken livers
1/2 cup clarified butter
1 pound plus 4 ounces
  mushrooms, sliced
2 1/2 sticks butter, divided
14 ounces heavy cream
14 ounces port
2 large shallots, diced
1/4 bunch fresh thyme
1/4 bunch fresh rosemary
Salt and black pepper to taste

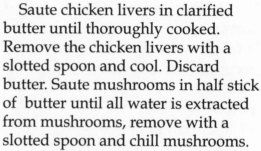

Saute chicken livers in clarified butter until thoroughly cooked. Remove the chicken livers with a slotted spoon and cool. Discard butter. Saute mushrooms in half stick of butter until all water is extracted from mushrooms, remove with a slotted spoon and chill mushrooms.

Reduce the cooking liquid left over from sauteing the mushrooms to about half. Add heavy cream, port, shallots, thyme and rosemary and cook until sauce thickens. Chill this mixture. (Makes about 1 1/2 cups sauce.)

Press chicken livers through the smallest holes on a food grinder at least two times; pass two sticks of butter through the food grinder once or puree in a food processor or blender. Fold butter, mushrooms and heavy cream mixture into pureed chicken livers. Season to taste with salt and pepper. Pour into a buttered mold and chill for 24 hours for maximum flavor. When ready to serve, run container under hot water to unmold onto plate.

Makes about 12 servings.

This appetizer was created by chef Louis Perrotte, a master of French cuisine. His Le Coq au Vin restaurant is a model of what every French country restaurant should be.

Le Coq au Vin's Warm Chicken Liver Pate
Orlando

1 pound fresh chicken livers
½ cup milk
4 tablespoons diced onions
1 small clove garlic, diced
2 eggs
5 ounces rendered chicken fat
4 tablespoons whipping cream
2 tablespoons port (optional)
Salt and pepper to taste

Clean chicken livers by cutting off all pieces of membrane or fat. Soak livers in milk for 30 minutes and drain.

Place liver, onions and garlic in blender container and mix at medium speed. When thoroughly combined, reduce speed to low and add eggs one at a time, rendered chicken fat, whipping cream, port, salt and pepper.

Refrigerate mixture for 30 minutes. Pour pate into 5-ounce aluminum cups.

Place in shallow baking pan filled halfway with water and bake in 350 F oven for 40 minutes.

Serve warm or cold with toast points, chopped onions, capers, stewed tomatoes, pickles.

Makes 4 servings.

Test kitchen note: To render chicken fat, chop the fat into small pieces, add a little water and simmer in covered saucepan about 15 minutes. When cold, lift out the congealed fat and refrigerate until ready to use.

Serve this appetizer with thin slices of apples or pears and unsalted crackers.

Le Cordon Bleu's Baked Brie
Winter Park

1 medium carrot, diced
1/4 cup minced scallions
2 tablespoons minced shallots
1/2 cup sliced mushrooms
2 teaspoons minced garlic
1/2 cup sweet butter
Pinch of saffron
Pepper to taste
3 tablespoons grated Parmesan cheese
2 sheets puff pastry dough
1 egg, beaten (to wash and seal dough)
1 (2.2-pound) wheel of brie
Parchment paper

Place brie in freezer for about 20 minutes to firm.

Slice chilled cheese wheel in half horizontally to create two layers. Saute carrots, scallions, shallots, mushrooms and garlic in butter until tender. Add saffron and pepper and allow mixture to cool to room temperature. Fold in Parmesan cheese to seasoned vegetable mixture.

Place one layer of brie, rind side down, on puff pastry and spread vegetable filling over top, pressing mixture firmly with back of spoon.

Place second layer of brie on top, rind side up.

Brush brie with beaten egg and pull puff pastry around edges and seal. Do not be concerned if the cheese wheel is not completely covered by dough. Flip brie over and place on parchment-paper-lined cookie sheet. Decorate with extra pieces of pastry dough shaped into leaves and brush all exposed dough with remaining egg wash.

Chill brie in refrigerator for about 20 minutes. Preheat oven to 425 F. Bake brie for 15 minutes or until dough is golden brown. Allow to cool and serve at room temperature.

This tantalizing appetizer was named after an Ybor City restaurant. It is a breeze to duplicate in the home kitchen.

Pebbles' Spanish Park Thumb Bits
Orlando, Winter Park, Longwood, Lake Buena Vista

6 (1-ounce) beef tenderloin
  medallions
Salt to taste
Pepper to taste
2 tablespoons clarified butter
1 tablespoon chopped fresh
  garlic
6 large, round croutons or
  crisp dry toast circles
6 thick slices kosher pickle

Season tenderloins to taste with salt and pepper.

In a saute pan, sear meat quickly to medium rare in clarified butter. At last minute, add chopped garlic and saute briefly; do not allow to burn. Remove beef from heat.

Place medallions on croutons that are about the size of the beef. Equally divide the garlic-flavored butter left in saute pan over meat. Place a pickle slice on top of each and serve.

Makes 2 servings.

Chef Arch Maynard developed this delightful appetizer for Baby Nova. The Italian new-wave restaurant closed in 1990 but its reputation for wonderful food still lives.

Baby Nova's Carciofi Buonanoti
Winter Park

2 large fresh artichokes
Juice of 1 lemon
Salt and pepper to taste
1 pound raw shrimp, any size,
   shelled and deveined
1 egg white
2 ounces whipping cream
2 eggs, beaten
1 cup flour
2 cups bread crumbs
Vegetable oil for deep-frying
Red Pepper Mayonnaise
   (recipe follows)

Cook artichokes in boiling water with lemon juice for 20 minutes. Drain and chill.

Remove artichoke leaves and dry each one.

In food processor fitted with a steel blade, puree the shrimp. Fold in egg white, whipping cream, salt and pepper and continue pureeing a few seconds more.

With a teaspoon, put a small amount of the shrimp mixture in the base of each artichoke leaf. Dust artichoke leaves with flour, dip in beaten eggs and then in bread crumbs.

Refrigerate leaves for about 15 minutes.

Heat oil in a deep-fryer.

Deep-fry stuffed leaves until golden brown, about 2 minutes.

Drain and serve hot with Red Pepper Mayonnaise.

Makes 2 servings.

Red Pepper Mayonnaise

2 large red peppers, roasted
and peeled
Juice of 3 lemons
2 cups mayonnaise
4 ounces fresh garlic
Salt and pepper to taste

Place all ingredients in food processor and puree.

Adjust seasonings to taste.

Spoon red pepper sauce in center of a serving platter. Surround sauce with Carciofi Buonanoti and serve.

The original recipe for this dish called for romaine lettuce. After several Park Plaza Gardens customers requested that it be served on Bibb the chef obliged. However, the name remains the same.

Park Plaza Gardens' Oysters Romaine
Winter Park

1 head bibb lettuce, chopped
½ stick butter seasoned with
 garlic to taste
6 oysters removed from shell
 (shells reserved)
½ cup hollandaise sauce
Pinch paprika
Salt and pepper to taste

Saute chopped bibb lettuce in garlic butter until wilted. Fill six empty oyster shells with sauteed lettuce, top each with rinsed oysters.

Place oysters under broiler until edges of oysters curl slightly, about 2 minutes. Top each oyster with hollandaise sauce, sprinkle with paprika and salt and pepper to taste. Return to broiler until hollandaise sauce is browned.

Garnish with lemon wedges and serve immediately.

Makes 1 serving.

These shrimp rolls are a breeze to prepare and would make great party fare. The shrimp filling can be made in advance and refrigerated until ready to complete the recipe.

Nine Dragons' Shrimp Rolls
China Showcase, Epcot Center, Walt Disney World

1 tablespoon ground water chestnuts
1 tablespoon ground onion
5 ounces ground shrimp
1 egg, beaten
8 slices sourdough bread
Vegetable oil

Mix together ground water chestnuts, onions, shrimp and beaten egg.

Heat vegetable oil to 350 F.

Trim off crust from 8 sourdough bread slices; spread slices evenly with shrimp mixture. Roll bread slices and secure with toothpicks.

Deep-fry rolled bread in hot oil until lightly browned. Remove and drain on paper towels. Serve warm.

Makes 4 (2-roll) servings.

These crab appetizers are excellent served with either a Dijon mustard sauce or a tangy cocktail sauce.

Riverview Charlie's Crab Bites
New Smyrna Beach

1/4 cup unseasoned bread
   crumbs
2 pounds crab meat, picked
   over and finely chopped
2 tablespoons finely chopped
   onion
2 tablespoons finely chopped
   celery
2 tablespoons finely chopped
   red pepper
1/4 cup mayonnaise
1/2 teaspoon salt
1/2 teaspoon minced fresh
   garlic
1/2 teaspoon mustard
1/2 teaspoon paprika
Juice of 1 lemon
1 egg, beaten
Cracker meal
Vegetable oil for deep-frying

Combine all ingredients except cracker meal and vegetable oil. Form mixture into small 1/2-ounce balls, roll in cracker meal, shaking off excess.

Heat vegetable oil to 350 F.

Drop crab balls into hot oil and deep-fry for 30 to 45 seconds or until crab balls are lightly browned. Drain on paper towels. Serve hot with sauce of choice.

Makes 15 to 20 appetizer bites.

Soups

Egg drop soups are found in German, Italian, Greek and Chinese cookbooks. The following recipe is a traditional Oriental preparation.

Jin Ho's Egg Drop Soup
Altamonte Springs

6 cups chicken broth
2 teaspoons cornstarch
½ cup cold water
1¼ teaspoons sugar
1 teaspoon salt
2 eggs, beaten
Few drops of sesame oil

Bring chicken broth to a boil. Combine cornstarch and water and add to chicken broth. Reduce burner heat to medium-high.

Continue cooking, stirring constantly, until liquid is smooth and just slightly thickened.

Add sugar and salt to broth mixture.

While continuing to stir mixture, pour in beaten eggs very slowly.

Remove from heat when eggs form threads.

Add a few drops of sesame oil and serve.

Makes 6 servings.

This creamy concoction is a delicious showcase for flavorful mushrooms. Serve with salad of mixed greens and French bread.

Maison & Jardin's Exotic Mushroom Soup
Altamonte Springs

4 ounces each oyster, shiitake and cremini mushrooms, sliced (more readily available fresh mushroom varieties may be substituted)

1³/₄ stick butter, divided

1 small onion, medium chopped

2 ribs celery, finely chopped

1 teaspoon finely chopped garlic

¹/₄ cup plus 1 tablespoon uncooked wild rice

1 cup sherry

2 quarts chicken stock

2 ounces brandy

3 cups heavy cream

¹/₄ cup plus 1 tablespoon cornstarch dissolved in water

Salt to taste

White pepper to taste

Melt ³/₄ stick of butter and saute onion, celery, garlic and raw rice until onion is transparent. Stir in sherry and reduce for a few minutes, stir in chicken stock, bring to boil. Reduce heat and simmer, uncovered, 30 to 40 minutes, until rice is done but still firm.

In a separate pan, saute mushrooms in 1 stick of butter; deglaze pan with brandy. Stir into rice mixture and heavy cream. Bring almost to a boil and stir in cornstarch mixture; reduce heat, continue stirring until cornstarch is blended with other ingredients. Add salt and white pepper to taste. Simmer for 5 to 7 minutes. Serve immediately.

Makes 12 servings.

This zucchini-laced cream soup can be served as a hearty lunch entree. Lightly seasoned, whole-wheat bread sticks are a good accompaniment.

Garden Terrace's Cream of Zucchini Soup
Marriott's Orlando World Center, Orlando

10 ounces zucchini
1 tablespoon butter
¹/₈ teaspoon garlic
³/₄ small onion, finely chopped
¹/₂ teaspoon curry powder
1¹/₄ cups chicken stock
1¹/₄ cups half-and-half
Salt and pepper to taste

Wash zucchini; trim ends and discard. Cut zucchini into thin slices.

Melt butter in a saute pan. Add minced garlic and saute lightly. Add onions and cook until transparent. Add zucchini slices and continue cooking until vegetables are tender.

Mix curry powder, salt and pepper. Add seasonings to cooked zucchini.

Put zucchini mixture in a blender or the work bowl of a food processor. Blend on medium speed until smooth.

Combine half-and-half and chicken stock and heat in a saucepan. Remove from heat.

Gradually add stock mixture to zucchini mixture. Heat to a mere simmer; do not boil.

Serve heated or chilled.

Makes 4 servings.

If desired, increase the white pepper in this recipe to 1 teaspoon to give the bisque a subtle kick.

Gary's Duck Inn's Seafood Bisque
Orlando

½ cup flour
½ cup butter, melted
1 quart milk
1 teaspoon garlic powder
1 teaspoon salt
½ teaspoon white pepper
2 tablespoons butter
½ cup sherry
½ pound scallops, chopped
½ pound shrimp, chopped
½ pound crab claw meat, chopped
2 teaspoons monosodium glutamate (optional)

Combine the flour and melted butter to make a roux.

To make a cream sauce, put milk in the top of a double boiler. Add garlic powder, salt and white pepper. When milk is hot, add the roux mixture and stir to blend. Cover and cook on medium-heat until mixture thickens.

Melt 2 tablespoons butter with sherry in a saute pan. Add chopped seafood and saute for 2 minutes.

Add seafood and monosodium glutamate to cream sauce in double boiler, turn off heat and let stand at room temperature for 30 minutes to allow flavors to meld.

Reheat and serve.

Makes 6 to 8 servings.

For a lighter version of this soup, turkey sausage can be substituted for the kielbasa.

Big Fred's Spanish Bean Soup
Orlando

½ cup olive oil
2 large onions, sliced
3 or 4 ribs celery, coarsely
   chopped
2 carrots, diced
1 green pepper, chopped
2 large cloves garlic, chopped,
   or 1 teaspoon granulated
   garlic
1 (22-ounce) can garbanzo
   beans
1 (8-ounce) can tomato sauce
1 bunch parsley, chopped
1 teaspoon dried basil leaves
½ to 1 teaspoon sugar
Salt and pepper to taste
2 kielbasa or hot smoked
   sausages, sliced (optional)
1 quart chicken stock

Saute onions in olive oil until transparent; add celery, carrots, green pepper and garlic, stir well.

Drain garbanzo beans, reserve liquid. Rinse beans and add to sauteed vegetables, stirring enough to coat beans with olive oil.

Add balance of ingredients including reserved bean liquid. Bring to boil, lower heat and simmer 1 to 1½ hours or until tender.

Makes 8 servings.

This light, spirited tomato soup is chock-full of fresh vegetables and herbs.

Buena Vista Palace's Tomato and Gin Soup
Lake Buena Vista

½ cup diced onions
2 cloves garlic, chopped
½ cup butter or olive oil
2 slices bacon, chopped
1½ cups peeled, seeded and
  chopped fresh tomatoes
1½ teaspoons chopped parsley
1 teaspoon basil
1 teaspoon oregano
3 cups tomato juice
1½ teaspoons sugar
1½ teaspoons powdered
  chicken bouillon
Salt and pepper to taste
1 cup sliced fresh mushrooms
3 ounces gin

Saute onions and garlic in butter or olive oil until transparent.

Add chopped bacon and saute for another 2 to 3 minutes.

Stir in chopped tomatoes, parsley, basil and oregano. Add tomato juice and balance of ingredients except the sliced mushrooms and gin.

Bring mixture to a boil, add sliced mushrooms and boil 1 to 2 minutes.

Remove from heat and stir in gin. Serve immediately.

Wild rice and almonds give this soup a unique taste. To shave off a few calories, use turkey ham instead of regular ham.

Omni's Minnesota Wild Rice Soup
Orlando

1 cup well-drained wild rice, precooked in chicken stock until tender
1/2 cup diced ham
1/2 diced carrot
1/2 diced onion
1/4 cup sliced almonds
1/2 teaspoon ground thyme
5 cups chicken stock
1/2 teaspoon salt
Dash of white pepper
1/4 cup white wine
Heavy cream to taste

Roux:
6 to 8 tablespoons flour
6 to 8 tablespoons melted butter

In large saucepan, combine rice, ham, carrot, onion, almonds, thyme, chicken stock, salt, pepper and white wine. Blend and cook for about 15 minutes.

In a saucepan over medium heat, make a roux of flour mixed with an equal amount of melted butter. Cook for a minute or 2 to blend. Stir roux into hot soup a little at a time until broth is desired thickness. Add heavy cream to taste. Adjust seasonings if needed and serve.

Makes 4 servings.

OMNI ❧ INTERNATIONAL HOTEL

This recipe is a bit of a chore to prepare, but worth the effort.

Crackers Oyster Bar's Seafood Gumbo
Church Street Station, Orlando

6 ounces ham, chopped
3 tablespoons butter
½ cup diced onion
⅓ cup diced celery
⅓ cup diced green pepper
1 teaspoon minced garlic
1 jalapeno pepper, diced
1 tablespoon gumbo file
½ teaspoon fresh rosemary
½ teaspoon fresh thyme
½ teaspoon fresh oregano
1¼ quarts fish stock
18 ounces clam juice
5 ounces crab claw meat
6 raw oysters with juice,
    chopped
6 ounces shrimp, peeled and
    deveined
6 ounces scallops
8 ounces canned or frozen
    chopped clams
1 fresh tomato, peeled, seeded
    and chopped
6 ounces canned crushed
    tomatoes
½ pound okra, sliced
½ cup cooked rice
1½ ounces sherry
Tabasco sauce to taste
Salt to taste
Black pepper to taste
White pepper to taste

Brown roux:
¾ stick butter
½ cup plus 2 tablespoons flour

To make the brown roux, over low heat, melt ¾ stick butter, slowly stir in ½ cup plus 2 tablespoons flour. Cook, stirring, until mixture is bound. Place in 250 F oven for 30 minutes, stirring occasionally. Mixture will turn brown as it bakes. Remove roux from oven; set aside.

In a large soup kettle, saute ham in 3 tablespoons butter until golden. Add onions, celery, green pepper, garlic, jalapeno, gumbo file and fresh herbs. Cook until onions and celery are transparent.

Add fish stock and clam juice; bring to a simmer. Thicken with brown roux, stirring well to incorporate; add all seafood, fresh tomato, crushed tomatoes and okra.

Simmer 45 minutes, stir in cooked rice and sherry.

Season to taste with Tabasco sauce, salt, white and black pepper.

Makes about 1 gallon.

Test kitchen note: This gumbo freezes well for up to 3 months.

The key to this recipe's success is the Havarti cheese. Mozzarella can be substituted, if desired.

The Garden Patch's Tomato Macaroni Soup
Orlando

Vegetable oil
3 pounds fresh mushrooms, sliced
3 very large onions, chopped
3 very large green peppers, chopped
3 tablespoons paprika
6 tablespoons garlic powder
6 tablespoons Italian seasoning
2 (46-ounce) cans tomato juice
1 (6-pound, 8-ounce) can diced tomatoes
Salt and pepper to taste
2 cups uncooked elbow macaroni
2 pounds Havarti cheese, cut in chunks or grated
1 to 2 cups grated Parmesan cheese

Saute the mushrooms, onions, green peppers, paprika, garlic powder and Italian seasoning in a small amount of vegetable oil.

In a large bowl, add sauteed ingredients to diced tomatoes and tomato juice. Cover mixture and refrigerate overnight.

When ready to serve, cook macaroni according to package directions, drain.

Put refrigerated vegetable mixture in large kettle, stir in cooked macaroni. Warm mixture over medium heat. Turn heat down to low and stir in grated Havarti cheese. Stir until cheese melts. Stir in grated Parmesan to taste.

Add salt and pepper to taste.
Makes 6 to 8 quarts.

Test kitchen note: Decrease the Italian seasoning to 3 to 4 tablespoons, if desired.

Black beans have long been popular in Mexico, Central America, South America, the Caribbean and the Southern United States. The cream-colored flesh of the beans has a mild, sweet flavor.

Big Fred's Black Bean Soup with Marinated Rice
Orlando

1 pound black beans
2 quarts water
1½ tablespoons salt
5 cloves garlic, crushed
2 tablespoons red-wine
  vinegar
1½ teaspoons cumin
1½ teaspoons oregano
5 ounces olive oil
1 large onion, chopped
1 large green pepper, seeded
  and chopped
1 green onion, chopped for
  garnish (optional)
Marinated Rice (recipe
  follows)

Wash black beans. Place in a large saucepan, cover with water and soak overnight.

The next day, add salt and bring to boil over medium heat (do not change water). Cover and simmer, stirring occasionally, until beans are soft, about 1½ hours. Remove cooked beans from heat and set aside.

In a small bowl, combine garlic, red-wine vinegar, cumin and oregano; set aside.

Heat olive oil in a heavy skillet.

Add chopped onion and green pepper, saute until onions are golden. Stir in garlic mixture, saute 1 or 2 minutes more. Add sauteed mixture to reserved beans; simmer for 1 hour, stirring occasionally.

To serve, place a generous tablespoon of Marinated Rice in the bottom of a soup bowl. Fill bowl with black bean soup.

Garnish with chopped green onion. Makes 4 to 6 servings.

Marinated Rice

1 cup cooked rice
2 tablespoons finely chopped
onion
2 tablespoons red-wine vinegar
1 tablespoon olive oil

Combine rice with onion, red-wine vinegar and olive oil.

Mix well and cover.

Let marinate at room temperature for 2 to 3 hours before serving.

Gazpacho is a refreshing chilled soup that originated in southern Spain. It makes a perfect warm-weather menu item.

Glen Abbey's Gazpacho
DeLand

1 large cucumber
2 fresh tomatoes, blanched
  and peeled
$^1/_2$ large green bell pepper,
  seeded
$^1/_4$ large Spanish onion
1 rib celery
1 garlic clove
1 cup tomato juice
$^1/_8$ cup white-wine vinegar
$^1/_8$ cup fresh lemon juice
$^1/_8$ cup olive oil
$^1/_8$ cup chopped pimento
$^1/_8$ cup chopped Italian parsley
$^1/_8$ teaspoon Tabasco sauce
Dash Worcestershire sauce
Salt and pepper to taste
Chopped green pepper,
  watercress, chopped chives
  or parsley for garnish

In food processor or by hand, chop cucumber, tomatoes, green pepper, onion, celery and garlic clove. Place chopped vegetables and balance of ingredients in a blender and blend to a thick pureed consistency, about 15 to 25 seconds. Add salt and pepper to taste.

Chill thoroughly, garnish and serve.

Makes 5 servings.

Crushed fresh garlic and a hint of rosemary leaves make this soup a special treat. Serve it with slices of marinated London broil for a complete meal.

Catering by Jenny's Cream of Mushroom Soup
Mount Dora

2 tablespoons butter
1 pound fresh mushrooms, wiped clean and sliced
3 cups chicken broth
3 cups heavy cream
Roux of 6 tablespoons flour stirred into 6 tablespoons melted butter
2 cloves fresh garlic, crushed
2 teaspoons rosemary leaves
Salt and freshly ground white pepper to taste

Saute mushrooms in butter until liquid is absorbed; set aside.

In a saucepan, heat chicken broth and heavy cream. Stir in roux; continue stirring over medium heat until liquid begins to thicken.

Add garlic, rosemary leaves (if dried, rub first between hands), mushrooms, salt and pepper. Simmer for 15 to 20 minutes.

Makes 12 servings.

The preparation of this soup can be a little tricky so follow chef Tony Pace's directions carefully.

Pebbles' Dijon Chicken Florentine Soup
Lake Buena Vista, Winter Park, Orlando, Longwood

1 gallon chicken stock or
   undiluted broth
⅓ pound butter
⅓ pound flour
1 tablespoon dry mustard
1 cup Dijon mustard
1 bay leaf
1 tablespoon salt
1 teaspoon white pepper
1 teaspoon granulated garlic
¼ cup Maggi seasoning
   (available in most
   supermarket gourmet sections
   and in Oriental markets)
6 dashes Tabasco sauce
1 pound fresh spinach leaves,
   cleaned and chopped
1 pint half-and-half
1 pound chicken breast

Bring chicken stock to a boil, return to simmer, add chicken breast and poach until done.

Remove from heat, remove chicken from stock and cool. Set stock aside and allow to cool.

In a stockpot, melt butter and stir in flour. Blend well. Cook slowly over low heat for 30 to 45 minutes making a pale roux. Stir in dry mustard. Add cooled stock to medium-hot roux, stirring with whisk and scraping edges with rubber spatula. Bring to a boil and quickly return to simmer. Stir in seasonings. Simmer for 1 hour, skimming any foam that forms; strain through a fine mesh. Skin, debone and dice cooled chicken; add spinach and diced chicken to soup base and simmer 10 minutes. Add half-and-half, return to simmer and remove from heat.

Makes about 1 gallon.

Test kitchen note: If soup is to be frozen for a short time before serving, do not add spinach until ready to serve. Simmer thawed soup with spinach for 10 minutes and serve.

This soup is a meal in itself. Add this to a tailgate party menu or serve to armchair quarterbacks on a rainy afternoon.

The British Shoppe's Cream of Potato Soup
Winter Park

1 pound (4 medium) potatoes,
  peeled and cut in chunks
2 cups chicken stock
1 cup milk
1 rib celery, finely diced
1 small carrot, finely diced
2 green onions, finely diced
Salt and pepper to taste
2 strips crisp bacon (optional)

Cook potatoes in water to cover until very tender and pieces begin to fall apart; strain.

Place potatoes in blender or food processor with stock; blend until smooth. Stir in milk. If necessary, add additional stock to reach desired consistency.

Lightly cook finely diced celery, carrot and green onion in salted water. Drain and stir vegetables into soup mixture. Season to taste.

Heat soup to serving temperature and garnish with crumbled bacon.

Makes 4 to 5 servings.

Jim Park developed this recipe for his popular Daytona Beach eatery. Park's Seafood Restaurant specializes in fresh seafood, gator tail and live Maine lobster.

Park's Seafood Restaurant's Fish Chowder
Daytona Beach

1½ cups vegetable oil
2 cups diced onion
1 cup diced green pepper
2 cups diced carrots
1 cup diced celery
4 tablespoons chicken base or chicken bouillon
1 tablespoon ground oregano
1 tablespoon diced fresh garlic or garlic powder
1 teaspoon ground sage
1 teaspoon ground thyme
5 drops Tabasco sauce
1 (16-ounce) can tomato sauce
1 (16-ounce) can crushed tomato puree
7 cups water
1½ pounds boneless fresh white, non-oily fish such as grouper or tile, cut in small pieces

In medium kettle, saute vegetables in oil until tender. Add remaining ingredients except fish; bring to boil, stirring occasionally. Reduce heat and simmer 20 minutes. Add fish and simmer another 20 to 25 minutes.
Makes 8 to 10 servings.

Great Northern beans have a delicate, distinctive flavor. They are grown in the Midwest and generally are available dried.

Brierpatch's White Bean and Ham Soup
Winter Park

1½ pounds dried great
  Northern beans
Water to cover beans
1 pound bacon, sliced and cut
  into ½-inch lengths
2 cloves garlic, minced
1 large onion, chopped
4 ribs celery, chopped into
  ½-inch lengths
1 red bell pepper, finely
  chopped
8 cups water
1 ham bone
2½ pounds ham hocks
2 carrots, grated
4 tablespoons fresh chopped
  parsley
½ cup dry white wine
½ teaspoon cayenne pepper
Salt and white pepper to taste

Rinse beans thoroughly with cold water. Allow beans to soak overnight according to package directions.

Drain beans.

Cook bacon until crisp. Drain bacon, reserving 4 tablespoons of the drippings.

Put bacon drippings in a Dutch oven or stockpot. Add garlic, onion, celery and red pepper and saute until vegetables are tender.

Add 8 cups of water, ham bone, ham hocks, carrots, parsley, beans, wine and bring to a boil. Reduce heat and simmer for 2 hours or until ham and beans are tender.

Remove ham when cooked and shred; set aside. Discard ham bone. Remove half of the cooked mixture and puree in batches in a blender or food processor. Return pureed mixture to Dutch oven. Add cooked bacon, shredded ham and cayenne pepper.

If thicker soup is desired, thicken with 2 tablespoons cornstarch that has been dissolved in a small amount of cold water. Season to taste with salt and white pepper.

Makes 8 to 10 servings.

This cream of mushroom soup is a classic French creation that can be served as a delicate first course for any meal.

La Normandie's Creme de Champignons
Orlando

4 tablespoons butter
1 pound jumbo mushrooms, sliced
1 medium onion, sliced
4 cups chicken stock
2 cups heavy whipping cream

Roux:
10 tablespoons butter
10 tablespoons flour

In a stockpot, melt 4 tablespoons butter. Add sliced onions and mushrooms and brown lightly. Add chicken stock. Cover and cook slowly for 1 hour. Coarsely chop mixture in a food processor or blender in batches. Be careful not to puree.

Return liquid to pot.

Prepare roux in separate pan by melting butter and blending in flour; mix well. Add roux to stockpot. Stir in whipping cream. Blend ingredients together well and cook over low heat for 30 minutes, stirring occasionally.

Makes 8 servings.

Who says the flavors of bacon, lettuce and tomato have to come together between two slices of bread? Add this delicious soup to a Sunday brunch menu.

Bay Hill Club's BLT Soup
Orlando

1 pound bacon, uncooked, cut into ¼-inch pieces
1 tablespoon butter
½ medium head romaine lettuce, cut into ¼-inch pieces
¾ cup diced onions
1 (32-ounce) can tomatoes, chopped
1 gallon chicken stock
3 tablespoons chicken base
1 bay leaf
1 tablespoon finely chopped fresh garlic
1 stick butter
1 cup all-purpose flour
2 cups half-and-half

Saute bacon pieces until brown. Drain grease and set aside.

In a stockpot, saute onion and romaine in a small amount of butter for 7 minutes. Add tomatoes, chicken stock, browned bacon, chicken base, bay leaf and garlic. Bring to a boil, reduce heat and simmer 1 hour.

In another pan, melt butter and stir in flour to make a roux. Cook and stir mixture over low heat for 5 minutes. Add roux slowly to soup and continue stirring. Cook mixture for 5 minutes. Add half-and-half and simmer slowly for 10 minutes. Add salt and pepper to taste.

Makes 18 servings.

Test kitchen note: This soup can be frozen for later use. Chicken base is available at some gourmet specialty shops.

THE BAY HILL CLUB AND LODGE

Pebbles' executive sous chef John Palinski created this conch chowder. Conch can be purchased fresh or frozen in supermarkets or fish markets.

Pebbles' Conch Chowder
Longwood, Winter Park, Orlando, Lake Buena Vista

2 pounds conch meat
1 small head green cabbage, diced
4 ribs celery, diced
3 medium carrots, diced
2 cloves garlic, chopped fine
3 slices bacon, diced
2 cups diced onion
½ cup olive oil
4 (8-ounce) bottles clam juice
2 (14½-ounce) cans chicken broth
6 cups water from conch cooking liquid
1 (1-pound, 12-ounce) can crushed tomatoes
1 (6-ounce) can tomato paste
2 tablespoons Old Bay seasoning
1 tablespoon Tabasco sauce
2 teaspoons black pepper
1 tablespoon Spike seasoning (available in health-food stores)
3 tablespoons leaf oregano
1 cup diced green pepper
1 red pepper, diced
1 (16-ounce) can diced tomatoes
1 (15½-ounce) can kidney beans, drained
2 cups diced potatoes
1 bunch green onions, chopped
Salt and pepper to taste
Additional Tabasco to taste

Place conch meat in a pot large enough to hold at least 6 cups of water, cover conch meat with water, bring to a boil and let stand, covered, for about 20 minutes. With a slotted spoon, remove conch and chill; reserve liquid for use in chowder. When conch is cool enough to handle, grind meat in a food processor or meat grinder until finely chopped; set aside.

In a large soup or stockpot, saute bacon a few minutes. Add olive oil, garlic and onion and saute until onion is transparent. Stir is a celery, carrots and cabbage and saute a few minutes.

Add clam juice, chicken broth and reserved conch cooking liquid.

Bring to a boil and add crushed tomatoes, tomato paste, Old Bay seasoning, Tabasco, black pepper, Spike, oregano and reserved ground conch meat. Simmer for 30 minutes and stir in diced green and red pepper, diced tomatoes and kidney beans.

Return mixture to a boil, reduce heat and simmer for 1 hour. Stir in diced potatoes and chopped green onion during the last 30 minutes of cooking time. Adjust seasoning with salt, pepper and additional Tabasco to taste.

Makes 1½ to 1¾ gallons.

Test kitchen note: This flavorful chowder freezes well.

Years ago Bailey's chef began offering this soup to employees on payday. One of the bartenders began calling the concoction Paycheck Soup and the name stuck.

Bailey's Paycheck Soup
Winter Park

2 quarts light chicken stock
2 bunches broccoli, florets roughly cut, stems reserved
1 large onion, diced
1 pound smoked ham, diced
1 pound uncooked turkey or chicken, diced
1 pound fresh Parmesan cheese, grated
1 banana pepper, diced
1 red pepper, diced
¼ cup chopped fresh parsley
1 bunch green onions, chopped
1½ pints heavy cream
Salt and pepper to taste
Dash of cayenne pepper

Roux:
1 cup clarified margarine
1 cup flour

To make roux, in skillet stir flour into margarine. Cook over medium heat, stirring constantly, for 15 minutes; set aside.

Clean and prepare vegetables, reserving broccoli stems, onion skin and pepper seeds.

In large stockpot, bring chicken stock to a boil with the reserved vegetable scraps; strain mixture.

To strained stock, stir in rough-cut broccoli florets, diced chicken or turkey and peppers; bring to a boil.

In a separate saucepan, saute onions and diced ham until onions are transparent and ham lightly browned. Stir into stock. Slowly add roux, half at a time, stirring. Watch consistency while stirring. Stock should just be slightly thick. If it becomes too thick, set balance of roux aside for another use.

Stir in heavy cream and return stock to simmer. Add Parmesan, chopped green onions and parsley. Simmer 10 to 15 minutes. Add salt and pepper to taste and a pinch of cayenne pepper. Remove from heat and serve.

Makes 11 servings.

Test kitchen note: Banana peppers are also called Hungarian yellow wax peppers.

Short ribs are very tough and require long, moist heat to cook. This hearty brew cooks them to perfection.

Ronnie's Cabbage Soup
Orlando

8 short ribs
3 medium onions, chopped
1 small head of cabbage, cut into pieces
4 medium tomatoes, chopped
6 cups water
1 cup sugar
4 teaspoons garlic powder
4 tablespoons lemon juice
1/4 teaspoon salt
4 ounces tomato ketchup

In a large stockpot, sear ribs. When meat is well-seared, remove from the pot.

Add onions, cabbage and tomatoes to drippings left in stockpot. Cook vegetables until soft.

Put meat back into pot and add the remaining ingredients. Simmer over medium heat for 2¹/₂ hours.

Makes 8 servings.

Test kitchen note: Ronnie's owner Larry Leckart calls this recipe Grandmother Hap Linches' Sweet-Sour Old-Fashioned Cabbage Soup With Flanken. It's a little different from the one served at the restaurant.

This exotic bisque is a perfect starter for a special occasion dinner at home. Serve with thin slices of garlic-seasoned French bread.

Maison & Jardin's Escargot Bisque
Altamonte Springs

1 quart beef consomme
4 tablespoons flour mixed
   with 4 tablespoons melted
   butter for roux
1 bunch scallions
1 teaspoon finely chopped
   shallots
1 tablespoon butter
24 large snails
1 ounce brandy
½ cup heavy cream
¼ cup dry sherry
Salt and pepper to taste
Whipped cream
1 teaspoon chopped chives

Heat consomme and thicken slightly with the roux mixture.

Saute scallions and shallots in butter.

Chop 18 snails and add to the scallions and butter. Deglaze pan with brandy. Add thickened consomme and boil for 20 to 25 minutes.

Add heavy cream and dry sherry. Season mixture to taste.

Heat six remaining snails.

To serve, garnish each portion with a dollop of whipped cream. Place a heated snail on whipped cream dollops and sprinkle with chopped chives.

Makes 6 servings.

Choose firm cucumbers with brightly colored skins to make this recipe. Store whole cucumber, unwashed, in a plastic bag until ready to use.

The Swiss Inn's Chilled Cucumber Soup
Lake Mary

1 large cucumber, peeled and
  cut in pieces
2 small pickling cucumbers,
  peeled and cut in pieces
2 tablespoons lemon juice
3 tablespoons chopped onion
½ cup consomme
3 tablespoons sour cream
1 cup heavy whipping cream
Salt and pepper to taste
1 tablespoon chopped fresh dill
Medallions of cucumber for
  garnish

In bowl of blender or food processor, place cucumber chunks, lemon juice, chopped onion, consomme and sour cream and puree.

Pour into a chilled bowl. Blend in heavy cream and salt and pepper to taste.

Stir in fresh dill and serve cold with garnish of cold cucumber medallions.

Makes 4 servings.

This soup has an unusual flavor combination that is perfect for a fall brunch. Using a pumpkin shell for a soup tureen makes a dramatic presentation.

Citrus Club's Pumpkin-Cheese Soup
Orlando

1 (6- to 8-pound) pumpkin
1 cup toasted croutons
²/₃ cup grated Swiss cheese
²/₃ cup grated Parmesan cheese
Salt, pepper and garlic powder
   to taste
3 quarts heavy cream

Preheat oven to 425 F.

Cut top of uncooked pumpkin to make soup tureen. Set top aside; remove seeds.

Layer toasted croutons and cheeses in bottom of hollowed out pumpkin. Add seasonings and fill with cream. Put pumpkin in a large pan and bake for 2 hours.

Remove pumpkin from oven.

Let pumpkin sit for 5 minutes. Carefully remove lid to let steam escape. Scoop out pumpkin meat from inside walls and put into serving bowls. With a ladle, top pumpkin meat with soup liquid that remains in pumpkin shell and stir. If necessary, adjust seasonings.

Makes 6 to 8 servings.

The flavors of cantaloupe, honeydew and watermelon meld wonderfully in this chilled fruit soup. File the recipe for warm-weather cooking, when melons are less costly.

Hyatt Regency Grand Cypress' Three-Melon Soup
Lake Buena Vista

5 whole cantaloupe melons, divided
1 whole honeydew melon
¾ cup watermelon chunks, without seeds
3 (6-ounce) containers plain yogurt
1 ounce Coco Lopez cream of coconut
1 ounce white wine
1 ounce Midori melon liqueur
Salt to taste
Juice of lemon
8 whole strawberries
Mint leaves

Use 3 of the cantaloupes to make serving bowls. Cut them in half, scoop out seeds and trim the rim of the melon leaving ½ inch of meat on the perimeter; set aside.

Halve remaining cantaloupe and honeydew melons, discard seeds and scoop out meat in chunks.

Place fruit in blender container or food processor and blend at high speed until pureed; strain.

Blend in yogurt, Coco Lopez, white wine, Midori, salt and lemon juice.

Refrigerate mixture until serving time.

Serve in cantaloupe cups and garnish with strawberries and mint leaves.

Makes 6 servings.

This warm fruit soup takes advantage of the robust flavors of dried fruits.

The Gables' Scandinavian Fruit Soup
Mount Dora

½ cup minute tapioca
6 cups hot water
1 cup light or dark raisins
1 (12-ounce) package pitted prunes
1 (8-ounce) package dried peaches
1 (6-ounce) package dried apricots
1 stick cinnamon
4 cups apple juice

In a large saucepan combine tapioca and hot water, stir well.

Chop and add dried fruits and cinnamon stick.

Heat mixture to boiling, stirring occasionally.

Reduce heat and simmer until tapioca is transparent, 30 to 35 minutes.

Stir in apple juice.

Makes 10 servings.

This is a signature dish for Caruso's Palace. It is relatively simple to duplicate in the home kitchen, but it does take some careful pot-watching during its preparation.

Caruso's Palace Zuppa ai Quattro Formaggi
Orlando

¼ cup (4 tablespoons) butter
1 medium leek, washed
   and chopped, using both
   bulb and green top
1 cup diced white potato
1 quart chicken broth
16 ounces heavy whipping
   cream
16 ounces half-and-half
3 ounces shredded provolone
   cheese
3 ounces shredded Parmesan
   cheese
3 ounces shredded mozzarella
   cheese
3 ounces shredded Cheddar
   cheese
Salt and white pepper to taste
Garlic croutons for garnish

Saute leek in butter. Add diced potatoes and chicken broth and continue cooking until potatoes are thoroughly done and softened.

Pour mixture into food processor bowl or blender in batches and puree until creamy.

Place puree into top of double boiler. Add heavy cream and half-and-half. Bring mixture to a simmer over medium heat.

Remove from heat and stir in all of the cheese. Return pan to stove and simmer, stirring until the cheeses are completely incorporated.

Adjust seasoning with pepper; rarely will salt be needed depending on the salt content of cheese. Top portions with homemade garlic croutons.

Makes 10 servings.

CARUSO'S PALACE

This is an updated version of a classic watercress soup. The diced avocados give it a nouvelle cuisine touch.

Le Coq au Vin's Potato, Watercress and Avocado Soup
Orlando

¼ stick butter
½ medium onion, diced
1 quart chicken broth
3 medium potatoes, peeled and diced
9 ounces watercress with stems, chopped or sliced and washed
Salt and pepper to taste
1 pint whipping cream
Finely diced avocado for garnish
Finely diced onion for garnish
Finely diced tomato for garnish

Heat butter in saucepan, add onions and saute over moderate heat until tender. Do not brown. Add chicken broth, stir to blend and bring to a boil.

Add potatoes and cook gently until tender. Add cut watercress and simmer 5 minutes. Heat whipping cream.

Place soup in blender and puree until smooth, adding hot whipping cream and salt and pepper to taste.

Serve hot or refrigerate and serve as a chilled soup.

Before serving garnish with diced avocado, onion and tomato.

Makes 10 servings.

LeCoq AuVin

This bisque gets its warm, nutty flavor from sherry, a fortified wine that originated in southern Spain.

Straub's Fine Seafood's Lobster Bisque
Altamonte Springs, Orlando

½ gallon milk
½ cup lobster base (available at specialty gourmet stores)
1 (11.3-ounce) can frozen Maine lobster meat (available in seafood markets)
1½ teaspoons chicken base
1 teaspoon white pepper
½ cup flour and ½ cup butter for roux
¾ cup good quality sherry (not cooking sherry)

Thaw lobster meat, reserve drained juice.

In a saucepan, stir together reserved lobster juice, lobster base, chicken base and white pepper. Over medium heat, bring to simmer; stir and simmer about 5 minutes.

Heat milk in top of double boiler.

While milk is heating, dice lobster meat, remove any cartilage. Add lobster meat to milk, bring milk to a near boil, do not allow to boil. Stir in lobster base mixture.

In a saute pan, make a roux by stirring equal parts of flour into melted butter, stir well and continue cooking over low heat until roux begins to bubble, about 5 minutes. Do not let roux scorch.

Stir roux, a little at a time, into bisque mixture. Continue stirring until roux is incorporated and bisque is slightly thickened.

Add sherry, stirring well from bottom of pan. Remove from heat and serve.

Makes 8 servings.

Garlic lovers will love this bisque. Pre-grated Parmesan doesn't come close to freshly grated cheese. Don't substitute if possible.

Karling's Inn's Artichoke and Garlic Bisque
DeLeon Springs

2 tablespoons butter
1 cup onion, finely diced
¼ cup fresh garlic, finely
   chopped
2 tablespoons flour
2 quarts chicken stock
1 teaspoon fresh basil,
   chopped
1 (12- to 14-count) can
   artichoke hearts (not
   marinated), reserve liquid
1 pint heavy cream
Salt and white pepper to taste
10 slices French bread, toasted
½ cup Parmesan cheese,
   grated

Dice artichoke hearts; set aside.

Melt butter in a stockpot, add onions and garlic and saute lightly, do not brown.

Add flour, mix well, add chicken stock and simmer 30 minutes. Add fresh basil, diced artichoke hearts and the reserved liquid, simmer 10 minutes.

Add cream, salt and pepper and blend well.

Sprinkle French bread toast slices with Parmesan cheese.

To serve, float toast slices in bisque.

Makes 10 servings.

Grated carrots and chopped onions add a sweet flavor to this cream of chicken soup. Serve with a tossed salad.

Riverview Charlie's Cream of Chicken Soup a La Mee
New Smyrna Beach

2 (8-ounce) skinless, boneless
  chicken breasts, cubed
2 tablespoons butter
1 cup finely chopped yellow
  onion
3/4 cup grated carrots
1 1/2 cups finely chopped celery
1 teaspoon garlic powder
Pinch white pepper
Pinch celery salt
Dash of thyme
Dash of dry Italian salad
  dressing seasoning mix
1 1/2 quarts milk
2 cups concentrated chicken
  stock

Saute chicken cubes in butter for about 2 minutes; add celery, onion and carrot. Cook until vegetables are almost done.

Add milk and chicken stock, heat to 170 F, a heavy simmer.

Stir in spices.

(If desired, thicken to taste with a roux made of equal measures of flour and melted butter, about 4 tablespoons each.)

Makes 8 servings.

Pearl barley is a popular ingredient in soups and stews. It's readily available in health-food stores.

King Stefan's Banquet Hall's Beef and Barley Soup
Magic Kingdom, Walt Disney World, Lake Buena Vista

3 tablespoons margarine
3 medium-size onions, finely diced
6 ribs celery, finely diced
2 large carrots, finely diced
$\frac{1}{2}$ pound roast beef, cooked and diced in $\frac{1}{4}$-inch pieces
3 tablespoons beef base or beef bouillon
2 tablespoons chicken base or chicken bouillon
Salt to taste (omit if bouillon is used)
$1\frac{1}{2}$ teaspoons granulated garlic
$\frac{1}{2}$ teaspoon white pepper
2 tablespoons parsley flakes
5 quarts water

Barley:
$\frac{1}{2}$ pound raw pearl barley
2 quarts water
2 teaspoons salt

Bring 2 quarts of water mixed with 2 teaspoons salt to a rolling boil. Add $\frac{1}{2}$ pound raw barley.

Cook for about 20 minutes or until barley is soft. Rinse in a colander with cold water until starch is removed.

In a large stockpot, heat margarine and saute onions, celery, carrots, beef and shallots. When vegetables are tender, add 5 quarts of water, beef and chicken flavorings, salt, garlic and pepper.

Add parsley flakes and barley mixture and cook for an additional 10 minutes. Add more water if necessary.

Makes 17 cups.

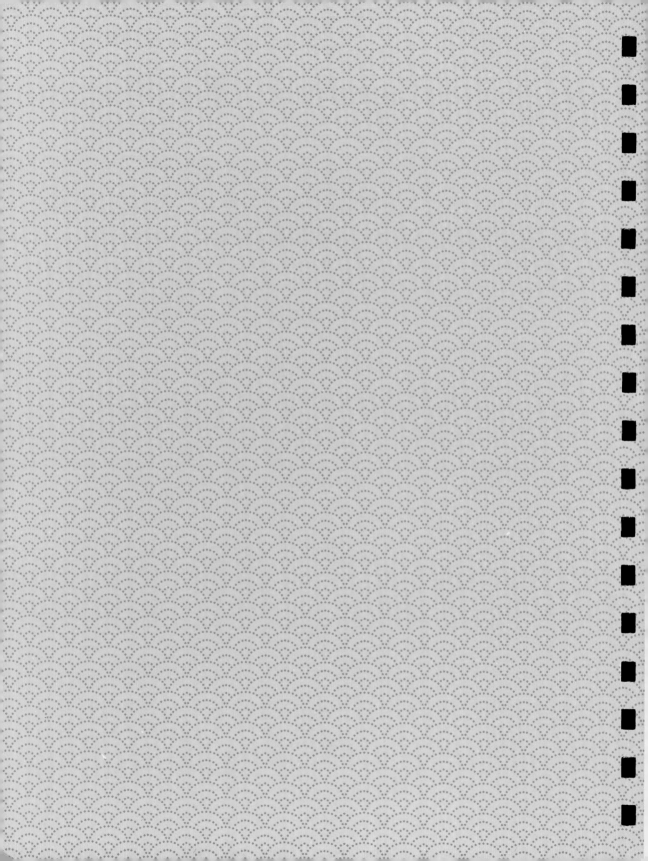

Salads &
Dressings

Freddie's Steak House has closed, but for years it was one of Central Florida's dining hot spots. The secret to preparing this salad: Rub the seasonings onto the sides of a wooden salad bowl and then scrape it all into the center.

Freddie's Steak House Caesar Salad
Fern Park

1 clove garlic
3 anchovy fillets
$\frac{1}{2}$ lemon
1 (1-minute) coddled egg
$\frac{1}{4}$ teaspoon dry English mustard
$\frac{1}{2}$ teaspoon oregano
4 tablespoons extra virgin olive oil
1 tablespoon red-wine vinegar
1 small head (2 handfuls) well-chilled romaine
$\frac{1}{2}$ cup seasoned croutons
5 ounces grated fresh Parmesan cheese
Freshly ground black pepper to taste

Grind garlic clove well into sides of bowl.

Cut anchovy fillets into small pieces and put in bottom of bowl. Squeeze lemon over fillets. Mash the anchovies to make a paste. Using the back of a spoon spread paste evenly over sides of bowl.

Break coddled egg into bowl. Blend in mustard and oregano. Add olive oil very slowly, whipping well with a fork to thicken. Scrape sides of bowl down to bring all of the seasonings into center of bowl. Stir in red-wine vinegar.

Put cold, whole leaves of romaine in bowl, cut leaves into bite-size pieces. Add croutons, Parmesan cheese and pepper to taste. Toss from bottom up until all leaves are coated. Serve immediately.

Makes 2 servings.

Test kitchen note: Eggs for Caesar salads are traditionally coddled. *The Joy of Cooking* (Bobbs-Merrill) offers this procedure: Lower an unshelled egg very carefully into boiling water. Cover the pan and remove from heat. Let the pan sit for 1 minute before removing egg and cracking into salad bowl. Generally eggs are coddled much longer before serving. Check an all-purpose cooking book for specific times.

Convenience foods combine to make this main dish. Use your favorite vinaigrette dressing recipe to lightly dress this salad.

Contemporary Resort Hotel's Tuna Macaroni Salad
Walt Disney World, Lake Buena Vista

2 pounds cooked macaroni
1 pound light chunk tuna, drained
1 teaspoon white pepper
1/8 cup diced red pimento
1/2 cup diced celery
1 cup vinaigrette dressing
6 hard-boiled eggs, chopped (optional)
1 cup mayonnaise (optional)
2 green peppers, diced (optional)
1 small onion, diced (optional)
1/4 cup finely chopped sweet pickles or relish

Mix all ingredients well. Chill for at least 1 hour.

Makes 15 to 20 servings.

Test kitchen note: Dried pasta usually doubles in volume when cooked; 1 pound dried pasta should equal about 2 pounds cooked. Fresh pasta changes little in volume.

This Chinese Pasta Salad is so flavorful it can be served without the dressing. Chinese noodles and hot chili paste are available at supermarkets and Oriental food stores.

Pebbles' Chinese Pasta Salad
Longwood, Winter Park, Orlando, Lake Buena Vista

1 (10-ounce) package Chinese noodles

1 bunch green onions, green tops and bulbs, finely diced

¼ cup soy sauce

2 tablespoons olive oil

¼ cup red-wine vinegar

1 teaspoon, or to taste, hot chili paste

1 teaspoon granulated garlic

1 teaspoon diced fresh ginger

¼ red bell pepper, diced

1 tablespoon Spike (available in health-food stores)

Cook noodles according to package directions, drain and set aside. Mix balance of ingredients in bowl; gently toss into cool pasta. Serve on top of salad greens or use greens for garnish with avocado slices, nuts and orange sections. If desired, serve with Vinaigrette Dressing (recipe follows) or your choice of creamy dressings.

Makes 5 servings.

Vinaigrette Dressing

1 (8-ounce) jar Grey Poupon Dijon mustard

1 tablespoon dry mustard

4 tablespoons oregano

4 tablespoons granulated garlic

2 tablespoons paprika

½ tablespoon cracked black pepper

½ tablespoon salt

⅔ cup sugar

Scant ⅓ cup lemon juice

Scant ⅓ cup soy sauce

1 quart salad oil

2 cups red-wine vinegar

Blend mustard with dry mustard, add spices and lemon juice. Slowly and alternately whisk in soy sauce, oil and vinegar.

Makes about 1½ quarts; Dressing keeps well in the refrigerator.

For best results, use fresh shrimp not frozen when making this recipe.

Edibles Etcetera's Shrimp and Broccoli Salad
Altamonte Springs

1 large cucumber
1 pound large shrimp
1 bunch broccoli, washed,
  stems and leaves removed
  and cut into florets
4 teaspoons finely chopped
  fresh dill
1 cup sour cream
1 cup Chantilly Cream (recipe
  follows)
1 teaspoon Worcestershire
  sauce
2 drops Tabasco
1 teaspoon fresh lemon juice
Salt and pepper to taste
1 bunch watercress

Peel large cucumber, halve lengthwise and remove seeds. Cut each half into three equal sections, then into thin julienne strips. Crisp in ice water for several hours.

Cook shrimp in boiling water until just pink. When cool enough to handle, peel and devein shrimp. Rinse shrimp and put into a bowl.

Cook broccoli in salted boiling water until crisp-tender; drain vegetables.

To make the dressing, combine all remaining ingredients except watercress. Combine dressing mixture, shrimp and broccoli and chill.

When ready to serve, make a bed of watercress on individual salad serving plates. Top with the crisp julienned cucumber. Mound shrimp and broccoli salad on top of cucumber.

Makes 4 servings.

Chantilly Cream

½ cup mayonnaise
½ cup whipped heavy cream
Pinch of nutmeg
Pinch of sugar
Salt and pepper to taste

Mix all ingredients together until smooth. Use in recipes as directed.

Palazzo pasta is a mixture of spinach, tomato-basil and egg fettuccine or spirals. It makes a colorful presentation for a special-occasion lunch.

Edibles Etcetera's Pasta Primavera Salad
Altamonte Springs

¼ head broccoli florets
½ pound palazzo pasta
¼ cup olive oil
1 medium tomato, diced
1 small zucchini, diced
⅛ cup finely diced scallions
1 heaping tablespoon
   commercial pesto sauce
⅛ cup pine nuts, lightly
   toasted
1 tablespoon red-wine
   vinegar
Salt and pepper to taste

Steam broccoli florets until crisp-tender. Drain vegetables and set aside.

Cook pasta until *al dente*. Immediately rinse with cold water and drain well.

Toss pasta in olive oil. Add diced tomatoes, zucchini and scallions to pasta along with drained broccoli, pesto sauce, pine nuts and vinegar. Toss ingredients to coat. Season to taste. Serve at room temperature.

Makes 4 side-dish servings or 2 main-course servings.

This variation of chicken salad is delicately flavored with chutney, curry and coconut.

Park Plaza Gardens' Chicken Curry Salad
Winter Park

$^3/_4$ cup chicken, cooked and
  cubed
$^1/_2$ teaspoon curry powder
$^1/_2$ teaspoon chopped onion
Salt and pepper to taste
Lemon juice to taste
1 teaspoon toasted coconut
1 teaspoon chutney
1 teaspoon raisins or currants
Mayonnaise
Extra raisins and toasted
  coconut for garnish

Mix chicken with seasonings, chopped onion, 1 teaspoon coconut, chutney and 1 teaspoon raisins.

Bind ingredients to taste with mayonnaise.

Garnish with a sprinkling of raisins and toasted coconut.

Makes 1 serving.

PARK PLAZA GARDENS

There are countless recipes for coleslaw, but this particular version is a favorite of Bill Knapp's customers.

Bill Knapp's Secret Coleslaw
Locations throughout Florida

1½ cups salad dressing (not mayonnaise)
1 tablespoon plus ½ teaspoon prepared mustard
Pinch of salt
1 tablespoon plus 1 teaspoon granulated sugar
1½ pounds finely shredded green cabbage
¾ cup chopped carrots
3 tablespoons chopped onions

Whisk together salad dressing, mustard, salt and sugar. Refrigerate mixture until ready to add to salad.

Pour dressing over vegetables and mix until creamy and evenly blended. Refrigerate until served.

Makes 8 servings.

This coleslaw was inspired by the colorful, tangy slaw presented at Philadelphia's legendary Bookbinder's seafood restaurant.

Charlie's Lobster House's Coleslaw
Winter Park, Orlando

1 medium head cabbage, shredded
¼ cup diced green pepper
¼ cup diced red pepper
3 tablespoons white-wine vinegar
3 tablespoons granulated sugar
1 small carrot, diced
½ cup diced red onion
½ cup diced celery
1 teaspoon black pepper
2 teaspoons Good Seasons Italian Dressing Mix
1 cup Hellmann's mayonnaise

Mix all ingredients. Blend thoroughly. Refrigerate before serving.

Makes 6 to 8 servings.

CHARLIE'S
LOBSTER HOUSE

This salad takes some time to prepare, but it's well worth the effort.

Cascades' Oriental Chicken Salad
Hyatt Regency Grand Cypress, Lake Buena Vista

2 (10-ounce) chicken breasts, skinned and deboned
Soy sauce
1/2 cup julienned raw carrots
1/2 cup julienned raw snow pea pods
8 medium mushrooms, quartered
1/2 cup bean sprouts
Teriyaki sauce, chilled (see test kitchen note)
Rice-noodle nests (see test kitchen note)

Preheat oven to 350 F.

Dip chicken in soy sauce. Put in a pie tin or other flat pan and bake in oven until tender, about 15 minutes. Cool, then cut chicken in julienne strips.

Combine chicken with vegetables; blend in enough chilled teriyaki sauce to bind and moisten.

Serve in deep-fried rice-noodle nests.

Makes 4 servings.

Test kitchen note: To make **teriyaki sauce**, combine 1/2 cup soy sauce, 1/4 cup oyster sauce, 1/4 cup hoisin sauce and 1 tablespoon finely chopped fresh ginger. Bring to a boil. Mix 4 tablespoons water and 4 tablespoons arrowroot or cornstarch and add to hot mixture. Cook on medium heat about 10 minutes. Remove from heat, cool and refrigerate.

To make **noodle nests**, use cooked, chilled rice noodles (not fried noodles). Break up noodles and put enough noodles in an 8-ounce ladle to fill it halfway. Press a 4-ounce ladle on top of the noodles. In a deep pan, heat oil to 400 F. Lower ladles into hot oil and cook nest until crisp, about 15 seconds. Repeat for more nests.

Crisp romaine and iceberg lettuce strips hold up well with thin dressings like the one for this salad.

Citrus Club's Gourmet Salad
Orlando

1 cup olive oil
$\frac{1}{2}$ cup wine vinegar of choice
1 tablespoon minced garlic
1 teaspoon minced parsley
$\frac{1}{2}$ teaspoon oregano
1 tablespoon minced pimento
$\frac{1}{2}$ teaspoon salt
$\frac{1}{4}$ teaspoon pepper
$\frac{1}{2}$ cup tap water
2 tablespoons sesame seeds
Romaine lettuce, cut in
   $2\frac{1}{2}$-inch strips
Iceberg lettuce, cut in
   $2\frac{1}{2}$-inch strips

Combine all the ingredients except sesame seeds and lettuces in the order listed.

Prepare a salad bowl with equal portions of romaine and iceberg lettuces. Sprinkle sesame seeds on greens and add dressing to taste. Toss ingredients with salad tongs and serve.

Makes desired number of servings. Refrigerate unused dressing

CITRUS CLUB

This main-dish salad will add a Greek accent to any lunch or dinner menu.

Pebbles' Mediterranean Salad
Longwood, Winter Park, Orlando, Lake Buena Vista

Romaine lettuce
Iceberg lettuce
Greek black olives
Tomato slices, halved
Halved artichoke hearts
Red pepper strips, julienned
Greek peppers
Hearts of palm, sliced
Cubed goat cheese
Angel hair pasta

Mediterranean vinaigrette:
1 (8-ounce) jar Grey Poupon Dijon Mustard
2 tablespoons dry mustard
4 tablespoons oregano
4 tablespoons granulated garlic
2 tablespoons paprika
1/2 tablespoon cracked black pepper
1/2 tablespoon salt
2/3 cup sugar
Scant 1/3 cup lemon juice
Scant 1/3 cup soy sauce
1 quart salad oil
2 cups red-wine vinegar

Depending on the number to be served and on personal taste, toss together romaine and iceberg lettuces, Greek black olives, halved tomato slices, halved artichoke hearts, julienne red pepper strips, Greek peppers, sliced hearts of palm, cubed goat cheese and cooked, cooled angel hair pasta. Set mixture aside.

To make Mediterranean vinaigrette, blend mustard with dry mustard, add spices and lemon juice. Slowly and alternately whisk in soy sauce, oil and vinegar.

Makes about 1 1/2 quarts dressing.

The dressing in this salad also can be served over butter lettuce or chilled melon slices.

Radisson Hotel's Spinach Salad
Orlando

4 bunches spinach
4 large button mushrooms, sliced
2 hard-boiled eggs, grated
8 slices thick-cut bacon
1 medium onion, peeled and finely diced
1 teaspoon pure honey
2 teaspoons white vinegar
$\frac{1}{2}$ teaspoon Dijon mustard
$\frac{1}{2}$ teaspoon salt
$\frac{1}{2}$ cup water
$\frac{1}{4}$ teaspoon black pepper, ground
Scallion flowers and carrot curls for garnish

Pick over, trim, wash and drain spinach leaves. Cut bacon in $\frac{1}{2}$-inch strips and saute until crisp. Remove half the bacon, drain on paper towels and reserve. Add onions to bacon pan and saute with remaining bacon until golden brown. Add honey, saute 1 minute. Stir in vinegar, mustard, salt, water and pepper. Simmer for 30 minutes or until dressing begins to thicken. Remove from heat.

Divide spinach on 4 salad plates. Top each with 1 mushroom, sliced; $\frac{1}{2}$ hard-boiled egg, grated; divided reserved bacon; and a scallion flower. Top with warm honey-mustard dressing and serve.

Makes 4 servings.

Radisson Plaza Hotel
Orlando

Waldorf salad originated at New York's Waldorf-Astoria Hotel in the 1890s. The original version contained only apples, celery and mayonnaise, but later chopped walnuts were added to the recipe.

Empress Lilly's Waldorf Salad
Disney Village Marketplace, Lake Buena Vista

5 large apples, diced
2 tablespoons lemon juice
2½ cups chopped celery
Dash of cinnamon
1 cup mayonnaise
⅓ cup chopped walnuts
¼ cup heavy whipping cream
1 tablespoon sugar
1 drop vanilla extract

Toss diced apples in lemon juice. Combine apples with celery, cinnamon, mayonnaise and walnuts. Stir gently to blend.

Just before serving, whip cream, sugar and vanilla and stir into salad.

Makes 6 to 8 servings.

Any type of rice is suitable for this salad. Wild rice will add a rich, nutty flavor and white rice will simply showcase the ingredients listed below.

Polynesian Resort's Chicken and Rice Salad
Walt Disney World

$^1/_2$ cup raw rice
$1^1/_2$ teaspoons mayonnaise
$1^1/_2$ teaspoons sour cream
7 ounces Coco Lopez Cream of
    Coconut
4 cups cooked chicken, diced
$^1/_2$ cup shredded carrots
$^1/_4$ cup crushed or chopped
    pineapple
2 tablespoons diced and
    peeled canteloupe
$^1/_4$ cup seedless raisins
2 tablespoons chopped parsley
$1^1/_2$ teaspoons Worcestershire
    sauce
Salt and pepper to taste
Chilled cantaloupe halves or
    lettuce

Cook rice according to package directions; drain well so that rice is very dry.

Mix mayonnaise, sour cream, and Cream of Coconut. Add rice and stir to blend. Add balance of ingredients, except salt and pepper. Let mixture stand for 10 to 15 minutes.

Add salt and pepper to taste, refrigerate for at least 2 hours.

Serve chilled on cantaloupe halves or on a bed of lettuce.

Makes 4 to 6 servings.

This is a healthful combination of bulgur wheat and fresh vegetables.

Chamberlin's Natural Foods' Tabbouleh
Winter Park

2 cups bulgur wheat
1³/₄ cups boiling water
³/₄ cup chopped green onions
2 cups diced firm tomatoes
1¹/₂ cups chopped fresh
   parsley or fresh mint
1¹/₂ tablespoons ground
   coriander
¹/₄ cup olive oil
¹/₄ cup lemon juice

Soak bulgur wheat in boiling water 45 minutes or until all water is absorbed. Stir in all other ingredients. Refrigerate for at least 2 hours before serving.

Serve on bed of sprouts, fresh spinach or lettuce.

Makes 7 cups salad.

The rich, buttery texture of avocados balances nicely with the plump shrimp in this recipe.

Maison des Crepes' Shrimp Salad with Avocado
Winter Park

1 teaspoon dry mustard
1 lemon, juiced
½ cup sour cream
¾ cup mayonnaise
Dash of salt
Dash of white pepper
Dash of celery salt
Dash of Worcestershire sauce
3 pounds medium shrimp,
    cooked and chilled
1 cup celery, diced
Cantaloupe, avocado slices,
    tomato wedges, ripe olives
    and parsley for garnish

Mix mustard into lemon juice. Add balance of ingredients, except shrimp and celery, then mix well.

Add shrimp and celery and toss until shrimp are thoroughly coated with sauce. Refrigerate.

To serve, garnish salad with cantaloupe, avocado slices, tomato wedges, ripe olives and parsley.

Makes 8 to 10 servings.

Hearts of palm and flavorful exotic mushrooms make this an elegant first course.

Dux's Hearts of Palm Salad
The Peabody, Orlando

1½ pounds baby string beans, haricots verts preferred

4 to 6 ounces vegetable oil

⅓ pound butter

2 pounds fresh wild mushrooms (shiitake, chanterelle and oyster)

Salt and white pepper to taste

4 medium shallots, finely chopped

2 pounds hearts of palm, drained

½ cup Walnut Oil Vinaigrette (recipe follows)

Trim ends of beans and clean remaining vegetable. Blanch beans in boiling, lightly salted water for 3 to 5 minutes. Do not overcook; beans should remain crisp and green in color. Put beans in ice water for 1½ to 2 minutes. Drain on paper towel.

Heat ⅓ of the oil in an 8- to 10-inch skillet. Add a teaspoon of butter. The butter should immediately brown. Be careful the pan does not flame.

Add one variety of mushroom, salt and freshly ground white pepper. Saute until brown and crisp on outside but still moist inside. Just before removing mushrooms from pan, add ⅓ of the chopped shallots to sweat in pan to release their sweet onion flavor. Repeat for remaining varieties of mushrooms. Drain on paper towels.

Slice fresh heart of palm ⅛-inch thick and immediately toss with Walnut Vinaigrette to keep hearts of palm from turning brown. Mix mushrooms together and warm in oven. Mix beans with palm and add warmed mushrooms, salt, pepper and Walnut Oil Vinaigrette to taste. Mound preparation on decorative plate.

Makes 4 to 5 servings.

Walnut Oil Vinaigrette

1 egg yolk
Salt and white pepper to taste
2 teaspoons Dijon mustard
5 teaspoons red-wine vinegar
1 pint walnut oil (available in
gourmet stores)

In stainless steel bowl, whip egg yolk to blend smoothly. Incorporate mustard, salt, white pepper and red-wine vinegar. Add oil in a slow stream, incorporating liquid as you proceed. Unused vinaigrette may be refrigerated in a closed container for seven to 10 days. If it becomes too thick, add a little water or wine to thin.

Makes about 2 cups.

In this dressing, rich orange blossom honey is combined with the savory flavors of cayenne pepper and mustard.

Bakerstreet's Honey and Spice Dressing
Orlando

1 quart mayonnaise
³/₄ cup vegetable oil
³/₄ cup orange blossom honey
³/₄ cup mustard
¹/₂ cup apple-cider vinegar
¹/₄ teaspoon cayenne pepper
1 tablespoon onion salt

Combine ingredients and chill for at least 1 hour before serving.
Makes about 1¹/₂ quarts; refrigerates well.

 Spoon a tablespoon or two of this dressing over a spinach salad or serve on the side with grilled pork or chicken.

Bakerstreet's Hot Bacon Dressing
Orlando

¹/₂ cup sugar
¹/₂ cup red-wine vinegar
¹/₂ cup mayonnaise
¹/₂ cup bacon drippings

Heat bacon drippings until hot but not boiling. Remove from stove and add all other ingredients, mixing thoroughly (a hand mixer works well). Blend until all lumps of mayonnaise disappear. Refrigerate any leftover dressing.
Makes 1 pint.

Poppy seeds and Worcestershire sauce give this honey-mustard dressing variation its unique flavor.

Orange Blossom Gardens Country Club's Honey-Mustard Dressing
Lady Lake

1 cup mayonnaise
¼ cup prepared mustard
¼ cup honey of choice
3 tablespoons poppy seeds
Dash of Worcestershire sauce

Blend all ingredients together. Chill and keep refrigerated until ready to serve.

Makes about 1½ cups dressing.

Feta cheese has a zesty flavor that's a welcome addition to salads and many cooked dishes.

Raintree Restaurant's Feta Cheese Dressing
St. Augustine

2 cups mayonnaise
2 cups sour cream
2 tablespoons white wine
2 tablespoons wine vinegar
2 tablespoons Dijon mustard
1 tablespoon chopped chives
$1/2$ teaspoon sugar
$1/2$ teaspoon salt
$1/2$ teaspoon white pepper
8 ounces feta cheese, grated

Combine all ingredients except cheese in the work bowl of a food processor; run machine for 30 seconds. Mixture should be smooth. Crumble or grate cheese by hand and add to food processor. Using the pulse button or the on-off switch, mix cheese into mayonnaise mixture. This step shouldn't take more than 15 seconds. Cheese should still be slightly lumpy.

Makes $1^1/2$ quarts.

Serve this dressing over a salad of fresh greens or use as a dip for crisp, seasonal vegetables.

Straub's Fine Seafood's Creamy Garlic Dressing
Altamonte Springs, Orlando

1 quart heavy mayonnaise
12 ounces sour cream
$^1/_4$ cup freeze-dried chives
2 teaspoons prepared mustard
$1^1/_4$ teaspoons Worcestershire sauce
$5^1/_2$ ounces buttermilk
$3^1/_2$ teaspoons granulated garlic
$^1/_4$ teaspoon salt
$^1/_4$ teaspoon black pepper

In large mixing bowl, blend together all ingredients with wire whisk; refrigerate.

Makes about $1^1/_2$ quarts.

This is one of the most requested recipes from fans of the late, great Parvenu. The variations on the base dressing make this a versatile addition to the recipe file.

Parvenu's Mustard Vinaigrette
Altamonte Springs

4 green onions
2 tablespoons Dijon mustard
4 tablespoons red-wine
  vinegar
³/₄ teaspoon salt
¹/₄ teaspoon ground white
  pepper
2 cups soybean (not corn)
  salad oil
4 tablespoons red wine

In food processor bowl on high speed, puree green onions. Add mustard, vinegar, salt and pepper and blend briefly until mixture is well-blended.

While processor is on high speed, slowly add salad oil. Add red wine. Adjust salt and pepper to taste.

Test kitchen note: To serve with spinach, fold into base dressing the juice of 1 ruby grapefruit, ¹/₂ teaspoon freshly ground black pepper, ¹/₄ teaspoon salt and ¹/₂ cup heavy cream.

To serve with pasta, fold into base dressing ¹/₄ cup grated Parmesan cheese, 1 tablespoon chopped garlic and ¹/₄ cup chopped fresh basil.

To serve with seafood, fold into base dressing 2 chopped hard-cooked eggs, ¹/₄ cup chopped gherkins, scant ¹/₄ cup chopped capers, juice of 1 lemon, ¹/₄ cup chopped parsley, ¹/₂ teaspoon chopped garlic and ¹/₂ teaspoon chopped shallots.

This is a deliciously different dressing that can be served with fresh fruit or chilled seafood.

Hyatt Regency Grand Cypress' Banquet Menu's Sweet Chutney Dressing
Lake Buena Vista

3 cups mayonnaise
1 cup Major Grey's mango
    chutney
1 cup white wine
1 tablespoon curry powder
¾ cup lemon juice
Salt and pepper to taste
2 tablespoons honey

In a large mixing bowl, blend together the mayonnaise, chutney, white wine, curry powder and lemon juice. Season to taste with salt and pepper.

Stir in honey. Store in the refrigerator.

Makes about 5 cups or 12 to 16 servings.

HYATT REGENCY ❈ GRAND CYPRESS

The following dressing holds the record for the most requested recipe in the history of my "Thought You'd Never Ask" column.

Pebbles' Zucchini Sour Cream Dressing
Longwood, Winter Park, Orlando, Lake Buena Vista

2 eggs
4 cups salad oil
1 cup red-wine vinegar
¼ cup lemon juice
1 tablespoon Worcestershire sauce
1 teaspoon chopped fresh garlic
Pepper (about 2 turns of the mill)
1 tablespoon grated Asiago cheese (fresh Parmesan may be substituted)
1 teaspoon salt
2 tablespoons sour cream
1 large zucchini, grated
Louisiana pepper sauce to taste

To make mayonnaise, put eggs and vinegar in a food processor; blend until mixture doubles in volume, about 1 minute. With the machine running, pour oil in a thin, steady stream until mixture thickens. Scrape into another bowl and, in the order listed above, blend in balance of ingredients. Adjust seasonings.

Makes about 1 quart; refrigerates well.

Serve this dressing with fresh strawberries, honeydew or cantaloupe cubes or any combination of fresh greens.

Park Plaza Gardens' Poppy Seed Dressing
Winter Park

4 ounces (half of an 8-ounce carton or slightly less than a 4.4 ounce carton) plain yogurt
1 tablespoon honey
2 teaspoons poppy seeds
Juice of ½ lemon
Zest of ½ lemon

If desired, lightly toast poppy seeds for fuller flavor. Stir together all ingredients. Refrigerate for a few hours to mellow flavors.

Test kitchen note: Zest is the thin yellow outer skin of citrus peel. Use a zester to remove or carefully shave with potato peeler and trim into fine pieces.

 Pistachio nuts are rich in calcium, thiamin, phosphorus, iron and vitamin A. They make a delicious addition to sweet and savory dishes.

Park Plaza Gardens' Raspberry Pistachio Salad Dressing
Winter Park

1 cup sour cream
1 cup mayonnaise
¼ cup raspberry vinegar
1 tablespoon lemon juice
1 tablespoon finely chopped shallots
4 or 5 pureed fresh raspberries (if not available, substitute beet juice for color)
Salt and pepper to taste
Peeled and chopped pistachio nuts for garnish

Blend together all ingredients except pistachio nuts. Refrigerate until needed.

When ready to serve, spoon desired amount of dressing onto individual salads; top with peeled and chopped pistachio nuts.

Makes about 2¼ cups.

This flavorful dressing is poured liberally over the Villa Rosa's complimentary antipasto. Diners often sop up what's left with the restaurant's slices of crusty bread.

Gus' Villa Rosa's House Dressing
Orlando

1 cup white vinegar
$^{1}/_{2}$ cup water
$^{1}/_{2}$ cup red wine
$^{1}/_{2}$ cup lemon juice
$^{1}/_{4}$ cup sugar
$^{1}/_{4}$ cup dried oregano
$^{1}/_{4}$ cup dried sweet basil
1 tablespoon dried parsley
   flakes
1 tablespoon garlic powder
   dissolved in enough warm
   water to make paste
1 teaspoon black pepper
$^{1}/_{2}$ teaspoon cayenne pepper
1 large onion, finely chopped
Salt to taste
2 cups vegetable oil
1 cup olive oil

In large bowl mix vinegar, water, wine and lemon juice. Add sugar and stir to dissolve. Add rest of dry ingredients, onion and garlic paste and mix well with wire whisk or mixer. Stir in oils and mix well. Refrigerate.

Makes about $1^{1}/_{2}$ quarts.

This classic dressing can be served over salad greens of choice or as a sauce for fish or shellfish.

Empress Lilly's Green Goddess Dressing
Disney Village Marketplace, Lake Buena Vista

1 cup plus 1 teaspoon
 mayonnaise
1/2 cup sour cream
1 1/2 teaspoons lemon juice
1/3 teaspoon salt
1 drop Tabasco sauce
1/3 teaspoon Worcestershire
 sauce
1/2 teaspoon garlic powder
1/2 cup half-and-half
Dash of white pepper
1 (1-inch) strip green pepper
3 sprigs fresh parsley
1 green onion
1 ounce anchovies

In a large mixing bowl, combine mayonnaise, sour cream, lemon juice, salt, Tabasco and Worcestershire sauces, garlic powder, half-and-half and white pepper.

Finely chop green pepper, parsley, green onion and anchovies. Combine with mayonnaise mixture.

Makes about 1 pint.

This dressing can be served over a beds of fresh greens or used as a dip for vegetables.

Pebbles' Palermo Dressing
Longwood, Winter Park, Orlando, Lake Buena Vista

1 egg yolk
1 whole egg
1 quart olive oil
1 quart cottonseed oil
2 cups red-wine vinegar
1 ounce Worcestershire sauce
2 ounces Louisiana hot sauce
1 teaspoon black pepper
$^3/_4$ teaspoon salt or to taste
$^1/_2$ teaspoon dried oregano
$^1/_4$ teaspoon dried basil
1 cup grated Asiago cheese
$^1/_8$ cup ground fennel seed
1$^1/_4$ cups sugar
$^1/_2$ cup chopped fresh parsley
Spike and Maggi seasonings
  to taste

Blend well eggs and vinegar; continue blending while pouring in oils in steady stream until emulsified in thin mayonnaise consistency. Stir in balance of ingredients until thoroughly blended. Refrigerate for flavors to meld.

Makes about 1 gallon.

Test kitchen note: Spike is available at most health food stores. Maggi seasoning is available at most supermarkets.

This creamy dressing has a nice peppery bite. Drizzled over salad greens and fresh vegetables it's a delicious crowning touch.

El Conquistador's Pepper Cream Dressing
Mission Inn Golf and Tennis Resort, Howey-in-the-Hills

1 quart mayonnaise
$\frac{1}{8}$ cup grated Parmesan cheese
$1\frac{1}{4}$ cups half-and-half
$\frac{1}{2}$ (1-ounce) can black pepper
Salt to taste (optional) or
 $\frac{1}{4}$ cup monosodium
  glutamate but not both

Blend all ingredients well.
Refrigerate until ready to serve.
Makes about $5\frac{1}{2}$ cups.

MISSION INN
GOLF AND TENNIS RESORT

Entrees

The St. Cloud restaurant has closed but the Melbourne location carries on the Spinelli's fine dining tradition.

Spinelli's Shrimp Christina
St. Cloud

½ stick butter
1 clove garlic, peeled
1 teaspoon Dijon mustard
4 shrimp, peeled and deveined
3 tablespoons orange juice
3 tablespoons white wine
1½ tablespoons Grand
   Marnier liqueur, warmed

In a large saute pan, melt butter. Add whole clove of garlic and saute for about a minute. Add mustard and stir. Add shrimp and cook until done. Remove garlic clove. Add orange juice and white wine. Reduce heat to a simmer. Stir ingredients and add warmed liqueur.

Carefully flambe contents of pan by igniting with a long, tapered match at the edge of the saute pan.

Remove shrimp with a slotted spoon to serving plate. Spoon sauce to taste over shrimp.

Makes 1 serving.

This custard pie can be added to a brunch menu or paired with tomato soup for a hearty dinner.

Publix Gourmet Plus' Broccoli Custard Pie
Shoppes at Heathrow, Lake Mary

Non-stick cooking spray
4 cups cooked chopped broccoli
1 cup grated Cheddar cheese
6 eggs
3 cups heavy cream
½ tablespoon salt
½ teaspoon pepper
1 (8-inch) springform pan

Preheat oven to 350 F.

Wrap bottom and sides of springform pan tightly with foil.

Spray the inside of pan with non-stick cooking spray, place cooked broccoli in pan and sprinkle with grated cheese.

Beat eggs with heavy cream, salt and pepper and pour over broccoli mixture.

Place springform pan into a baking pan; fill larger pan with water halfway up the springform pan.

Place in oven and bake until top browns, about 15 minutes.

Cover with foil and continue baking another 45 minutes or until pick or sharp knife inserted in custard comes out clean.

Remove from oven and carefully lift broccoli custard pan out of water bath.

Makes 8 servings.

Serve this citrus-sauced entree with a crisp fume blanc or a chardonnay.

Jordan's Grove's Swordfish with Almond and Orange Sauce
Maitland

1 (8-ounce) swordfish fillet
  per serving
½ cup sliced or pureed
  almonds
1 stick butter
4 tablespoons flour
1 pint heavy cream
2 cups chicken stock
1 quart fresh orange juice

Saute swordfish fillets until nearly done. Bake fillets in oven at 300 F while preparing sauce.

Saute almonds until brown in small amount of butter. While pan is still hot, add remainder of butter. When butter is melted, stir in flour to make a roux. Stir in cream and heat, continuing to stir, until mixture begins to bubble. Stir in chicken stock and add orange juice. Reduce mixture by ½ (more if you're patient). Serve over swordfish fillets.

Makes about 1 quart.

Cooks in Malaysia and Hawaii have long treasured coconut as a recipe ingredient. Serve this dish with a simple rice pilaf and steamed green beans for a complete meal.

Bakerstreet's Hawaiian Fried Shrimp
Orlando

2 eggs
1½ cups milk
½ cup pineapple juice
½ teaspoon salt
½ teaspoon baking powder
1 (15-ounce) can Coco Lopez
  Cream of Coconut
2 cups flour
2½ pounds (21- to 25-count)
  shrimp
1 cup finely ground
  unseasoned bread crumbs
1 cup flaked coconut
Sweet Sour Orange Sauce
  (recipe follows)

To make batter, combine eggs, milk, pineapple juice, salt, baking powder and Cream of Coconut. Mix thoroughly. Slowly add flour while beating until mixture is smooth; set aside.

Peel, devein and butterfly shrimp.

Mix bread crumbs and flaked coconut for breading. Coat shrimp with batter, shake off excess.

Press into breading mixture. Place on tray and freeze until firm.

Heat deep-fryer to 350 F. Fry shrimp for 1½ minutes or until golden brown. (Always fry shrimp from a frozen state, not thawed.) Serve with Sweet Sour Orange Sauce.

Makes 6 servings.

Sweet Sour Orange Sauce

1 cup ketchup
¾ cup orange marmalade
⅓ cup red-wine vinegar
2 tablespoons soy sauce
2 tablespoons lemon juice
1½ tablespoons dry mustard
2 tablespoons horseradish
½ teaspoon curry powder

Combine all ingredients in a saucepan and heat until hot and bubbly. Serve warm with fried shrimp.

Chef Tony Alexatos has delighted diners through the years as executive chef in several Central Florida restaurants and through his catering service.

Chef Tony's Chicken Carolina with Pecan Dressing
Orlando

¼ cup melted butter
1 cup finely chopped onion
1 cup finely chopped celery
1 cup water
Dash black pepper
1 teaspoon chicken base
½ teaspoon poultry seasoning
¾ cup finely chopped cooked link sausage
¾ cup chopped pecans
½ cup half-and-half
5 slices white bread, cut into cubes
1 egg
5 (6-ounce) skinless chicken breasts
15 slices bacon
10 plain round toothpicks
Sauce (recipe follows)

Preheat oven to 350 F.

Heat butter in saute pan, add onions and saute for 3 minutes; add celery and water and cook slowly until celery becomes tender. Add dash of black pepper, chicken base, poultry seasoning, sausage and pecans. Stir in half-and-half and cook for 1 minute. Remove from heat and mix in bread cubes.

Stir in egg and blend until well-mixed. Let dressing cool before using.

Separate dressing into five equal portions and roll into ball shapes. Cover each dressing ball with one whole chicken breast. Using three strips of bacon for each portion, cut one strip in half and crisscross across top of chicken breast, using the two remaining strips to wrap around the sides of the chicken breast. Use two toothpicks to hold bacon strips in place on the sides.

Place chicken on lightly greased baking pan. Bake in preheated oven.

When bacon is crisp, chicken will be done.

While chicken is baking, prepare sauce.

This is a favorite dish in many Spanish-speaking countries. Variations reflect taste preferences in certain areas.

Numero Uno's Picadillo
Orlando

1 medium onion, peeled

1 medium green pepper, cored and washed

2 tomatoes

4 cloves garlic, crushed

2 tablespoons corn oil

1 pound very lean ground beef

3 tablespoons tomato sauce

2 tablespoons white wine

½ teaspoon cumin

Salt to taste

Black pepper to taste

½ teaspoon paprika

2 rounded tablespoons raisins (optional)

12 pimento-stuffed green olives, (optional)

½ teaspoon yellow food color (optional)

1 potato, peeled, cubed and deep-fried

Grind or finely chop onion, green pepper, garlic and tomatoes. Saute in oil until tender.

Add balance of ingredients except cubed potatoes. Simmer, stirring occasionally, 30 to 45 minutes.

Fold in deep-fried potatoes. Serve. Makes 4 servings.

Here's a healthful, meatless chili. Meat lovers can add ground turkey, if desired.

Vine and Harvest Shops' Vegetarian Chili
Altamonte Mall, Altamonte Springs

1 (2-pound) can Heinz tomato
sauce (or sauce of your choice)
1 (2-pound) can kidney beans,
drained
1 large green bell pepper
cleaned and chopped
1 medium onion, peeled and
chopped
3 fresh tomatoes, cut in small
chunks
1 carrot, cleaned and grated
8 ounces Danish havarti
cheese, cut in chunks
2 tablespoons mild chili
powder
1 tablespoon Spike (available
in health food stores)
1 tablespoon dried sweet basil

Mix all ingredients together in
large stockpot or Dutch oven. Bring
to a simmer and cook 1^{1}/$_{2}$ hours,
stirring occasionally.

Makes 8 to 10 servings.

This dish is crowned with a classic French bearnaise sauce. This rich, tarragon-flavored preparation also can be served on vegetables, meat and eggs.

Charlie's Lobster House's Flounder Oscar
Winter Park, Orlando

2 pounds fresh flounder cut
   into 8-ounce fillets
8 ounces snow or king crab,
   cleaned
24 thin asparagus spears, fresh
   or frozen, parboiled to
   al dente stage
White pepper to taste
Granulated garlic to taste

Bearnaise sauce:
$\frac{1}{2}$ cup dry white wine
10 whole black peppercorns,
   cracked
10 parsley stems
1 teaspoon dried tarragon
$\frac{1}{4}$ cup tarragon vinegar
Pinch of chervil, optional
1 tablespoon chopped shallots
2 egg yolks
6 to 8 ounces clarified butter
Finely chopped tarragon
   leaves for garnish

Portion flounder, brush with butter and place in buttered baking pan. Season lightly with white pepper and granulated garlic; set aside.

Preheat oven to 400 F.

Put first seven ingredients for bearnaise sauce in a pan over medium heat until mixture is almost dry, close to a glaze. When cool enough to handle, squeeze mixture through a piece of cheesecloth to yield about 1 ounce of liquid.

Add 1 ounce of seasoning yield to the egg yolks in a double boiler over medium heat. Cook mixture, whipping constantly until very thick. Remove from heat and slowly pour in clarified butter, whipping constantly, until all butter is incorporated. Garnish with chopped tarragon leaves.

Bake fish for 8 minutes. Remove from oven, place strips of crab on top of each fillet and two parboiled asparagus spears diagonally on each, with two more spears on the sides. Return to oven 1 to 2 minutes until crab is warm. Remove from oven, place each portion on individual serving dishes and top with bearnaise sauce.

Makes 4 servings.

This creamy, nicely seasoned cheese and spinach custard is one of the Runcible Spoon's gourmet specialties.

Runcible Spoon Tea Room's Florentine Tart
Longwood historical district

½ pound butter, melted
11 sheets phyllo dough
15 ounces ricotta cheese
½ cup grated mozzarella cheese
1 (10-ounce) package frozen chopped spinach
2 eggs
¼ teaspoon nutmeg
1 package Good Seasons cheese-garlic salad dressing mix (Italian mix may be substituted)

Preheat oven to 350 F.

Brush a 9-inch tart pan (with removable bottom) with butter. Layer with 8 sheets phyllo dough, brushing melted butter between each layer.

Thaw spinach and squeeze dry. Mix together ricotta, mozzarella and spinach.

In a small bowl, beat eggs and add nutmeg and seasoning mix. Stir custard into cheese and spinach mixture.

Put mixture into the tart pan and pull ends of dough over top to make a circle.

Butter 3 remaining sheets of phyllo and cover top of tart. Butter any dry spots with pastry brush.

Put tart pan on cookie sheet and bake 30 minutes. Cool slightly before cutting into wedges.

Makes 6 servings.

This light and colorful dish is one of the Hyatt's "Perfect Balance Meals," a selection of low-calorie, low-cholesterol menu items.

Cascade's Stir-Fry Chicken and Shrimp Sesame
Hyatt Regency Grand Cypress, Lake Buena Vista

¼ **pound broken shrimp pieces**
¼ **pound boneless breast of chicken cut in 1/4-inch-by-3-inch strips**
1 **tablespoon margarine**
½ **cup pea pods**
½ **cup button mushrooms**
1 **leaf bok choy, sliced**
½ **cup bean sprouts**
Teriyaki Sauce (recipe follows)
Sesame seeds
Chopped green onion for garnish

In a wok or pan over medium-high heat, saute seafood and chicken in margarine for 3 minutes. Add Oriental vegetables and cook 3 minutes longer, stirring constantly while adding Teriyaki Sauce. To serve on plate, sprinkle each portion with sesame seeds; garnish with chopped green onions.

Makes 2 servings.

Teriyaki Sauce

2 **teaspoons minced garlic**
¼ **cup gin**
1 **teaspoon ginger, unpeeled and finely chopped**
1 **tablespoon sugar**
½ **cup soy sauce**
½ **cup oyster sauce**

Saute minced garlic until transparent, add gin and reduce by one-third. Add ginger, sugar, soy sauce and oyster sauce. Bring to a boil. Reduce heat and simmer 5 minutes.

This dish is named for the harbor city of Rimini on the Northern Italian Adriatic coast.

Christini's Fettuccine alla Rimini
Orlando

---

16 ounces fresh fettuccine
8 ounces smoked salmon
  sliced into small pieces
1 tablespoon butter
1 ounce vodka, warmed
1 cup heavy cream
3 egg yolks, beaten
1 cup grated Parmesan cheese

Cook fresh fettuccine to *al dente* stage; set pasta aside and keep warm.

Over medium heat, saute salmon with butter, add vodka and carefully flambe by igniting contents from the side of the pan with a long, tapered match.

Stir in heavy cream; reduce slightly to allow cream to thicken.

Add pasta; blend mixture well with egg yolks.

Remove from heat, stir in cheese and serve immediately.

Makes 4 servings.

CHRISTINI'S
RISTORANTE ITALIANO

Tart apples and robust sausage give this dish a wonderful flavor combination.

Omni's Stuffed Chicken Breast with Apple Almond Stuffing
Orlando

4 ounces Italian sausage
½ cup diced onion
½ cup diced celery
1 cup chicken stock
⅛ teaspoon sage or poultry
   seasoning
⅛ teaspoon thyme
⅛ teaspoon basil
Pinch garlic salt
½ cup diced green apples
Lemon juice
⅛ cup almonds
2 cups bread crumbs
6 (8-ounce) boneless chicken
   breasts
Melted butter
Salt to taste
Pepper to taste
Paprika to taste

Chop sausage and in a skillet saute until browned. Drain off all but 1 tablespoon drippings; add onion and celery and saute until limp. Add stock, sage, thyme, basil and garlic salt; bring to boil and continue boiling for 5 minutes.

While stock is boiling, dice apples into ¼-inch cubes; place in water with lemon juice to keep fruit from discoloring.

Saute almonds until light brown. Add crumbs to skillet; mix well. Drain apples and add to skillet. Add almonds and toss ingredients to coat. Remove pan from heat and let cool.

Lay chicken breast skin side down on wax-paper-covered counter or work board. Place equal portions of stuffing in center of each breast and fold chicken into an oval. Tuck in ends. Brush with butter and season with salt, pepper and paprika.

Place in lightly buttered baking dish, fold side down and roast in preheated 350 F oven for 30 minutes or until tender. (For this dish, it is best not to skin the chicken. The oil in the skin will baste the breast and keep it moist.)

Makes 6 servings.

These crab cakes are baked in a white wine and butter mixture. Add chopped green onions to the basic mixture for a spicier taste.

Hemingways' Maryland Crab Cakes
Hyatt Regency Grand Cypress, Lake Buena Vista

1 pound crab meat, cooked
½ cup mayonnaise
2 tablespoons Old Bay
  seasoning (available in most
  supermarkets)
3 eggs
4 tablespoons Worcestershire
  sauce
¼ cup bread crumbs
½ cup white wine
2 tablespoons lemon juice
2 tablespoons melted butter

In bowl, mix together eggs and mayonnaise. Add Old Bay seasoning and Worcestershire sauce and mix well.

In another bowl, gently break up crab meat, leaving whole lumps. Remove any shells.

Add bread crumbs and toss until crab meat is lightly covered. Add mayonnaise mixture and mix well.

Pour wine, lemon juice and melted butter in bottom of 9-inch-by-9-inch baking pan.

With a 3-ounce ice cream scoop form crab cakes and put into pan with white wine liquid. If you do not have a scoop, form small cakes with hands, about the size of silver dollar pancakes.

Bake at 350 F for 10 to 15 minutes.
Makes 4 servings.

HEMINGWAYS

The following crab cake mixture is deep-fried in the traditional manner.

Gary's Duck Inn's Baltimore-Style Crab Cakes
Orlando

½ cup melted butter
½ cup flour
3½ cups milk
1 tablespoon olive or peanut oil
2 ounces diced celery
2 ounces diced Spanish onion
1 ounce diced green pepper
1 pound lump claw crab meat, cleaned and cut in small chunks
1 teaspoon prepared mustard
1 teaspoon Old Bay seasoning (available in most supermarkets)
½ tablespoon Tabasco sauce
½ teaspoon salt
¼ teaspoon white pepper
1 teaspoon lemon juice
1 egg, beaten
2 cups dry bread crumbs
Equal parts flour and cracker meal for dusting
Vegetable oil for deep-frying

Make a white sauce by stirring flour into melted butter in pan over medium heat; slowly stir in milk until mixture is smooth; continue cooking, stirring, until mixture thickens. Remove white sauce from heat and reserve.

Saute diced celery, onion and green pepper in olive or peanut oil until tender; reserve.

In a large mixing bowl blend crab meat, beaten egg, sauteed vegetables and lemon juice.

Fold mustard and other seasonings into white sauce. Stir white sauce into crab mixture. Add bread crumbs.

Refrigerate 1 hour before forming into round, flattened crab cakes.

Heat oil to 350 F.

Lightly dust cakes with flour-cracker meal mixture and deep-fry until golden brown.

(Crab mixture is also good baked, broiled and stuffed into mushroom caps.)

Makes about 7 crab cakes.

Delicate strands of fresh angel hair pasta are gently seasoned with a traditional pesto blend in this recipe.

Enzo's Tagliatelline al Pesto
Longwood

1 ounce (1 to 1½ cups) fresh
  basil
1 rounded tablespoon Italian
  pine nuts
2 medium garlic cloves
2 ounces extra-virgin olive oil
1 tablespoon grated
  Parmigiano-reggiano cheese
  (available at Italian markets)
Salt and white pepper to taste
Fresh pasta (angel hair or
  tagliatelle) for 4 servings

To make pesto sauce, finely chop basil, garlic and pine nuts. Add olive oil, Parmigiano and salt and pepper; mix well.

Cook pasta to *al dente* stage and drain.

Add pesto sauce to drained pasta, toss gently and serve immediately.

Makes 4 servings.

Restaurant
on the Lake

Don't substitute dried for fresh Parmesan cheese. The dried versions generally include unwanted fillers like salt and additional fats.

Alfredo the Original of Roma's Pasta Alfredo
Italy Showcase, Epcot Center, Walt Disney World

½ cup butter or margarine
⅔ cup heavy cream
1½ cups grated fresh
  Parmesan cheese
¼ teaspoon salt
Dash pepper
Chopped parsley
12 ounces fresh pasta, cooked
  and drained

Heat butter and cream in saucepan until butter is melted. Remove pan from heat. Add 1 cup Parmesan cheese, salt and pepper. Stir until sauce is blended and fairly smooth. Add to drained noodles and toss until they are well coated.

Sprinkle with remaining Parmesan cheese and chopped parsley. Serve at once.

Makes 6 servings.

Here's a gorgeous entree for a special-occasion meal. Serve dinner guests a delicately seasoned hot and sour soup for a first course.

Nine Dragons' Kang Boa Chicken
China Showcase, Epcot Center, Walt Disney World

3/4 **pound boneless chicken breast**

1 egg, beaten

Salt and white pepper to taste

1 teaspoon cornstarch

3 tablespoons peanut oil, divided

10 dry hot peppers (available in Oriental groceries)

1/4 **cup green onions cut in** 1/2**-inch pieces**

1 tablespoon diced fresh ginger

1/2 **tablespoon finely chopped garlic**

1 tablespoon good-quality sherry (not cooking sherry)

3 tablespoons soy sauce

1/2 **tablespoon sugar**

1/4 **cup concentrated chicken broth**

1/2 **tablespoon white vinegar**

1 1/2 **tablespoons cornstarch**

1 1/2 **tablespoons water**

1 cup peanuts deep-fried until golden and crunchy

Cut chicken meat into cubes. Toss with salt, white pepper, egg and cornstarch. Set aside for 30 minutes to marinate.

Add 2 tablespoons oil to wok and tilt pan to distribute. When temperature reaches 350 F, add chicken and stir fry until almost done. Remove meat with a slotted spoon and drain on paper towels.

Dry wok and add 1 tablespoon oil, dry peppers, green onions, ginger and garlic. Stir-fry about 1 minute; add chicken and stir together. Add sherry, soy sauce, sugar, chicken broth, white vinegar and cornstarch dissolved in 1 1/2 tablespoons water. Stir in fried peanuts and stir-fry until chicken is fully cooked.

Serve immediately with white rice. Makes 2 servings.

Test kitchen note: At Epcot Center, the experienced Chinese chefs add the 2 tablespoons of oil to a wok that is preheated to 350 F. We altered the recipe for the home cook because splattering of the oil on a very hot surface may be dangerous to a cook inexperienced in working with a wok.

This flavorful dish is ready in no time thanks to the speedy cooking of the wok.

Nine Dragons' Saucy Chicken
China Showcase, Epcot Center, Walt Disney World

$3/4$ **pound boneless chicken breast**
1 egg, beaten
White pepper to taste
1 teaspoon cornstarch
3 tablespoons peanut oil, divided
$1/2$ **cup chopped Bermuda onion**
$1/2$ **cup thinly sliced carrots**
$1/4$ **cup fresh green peas**
1 tablespoon good-quality sherry (not cooking sherry)
3 tablespoons soy sauce
$1/2$ **tablespoon sugar**
3 tablespoons concentrated chicken broth
$1^1/2$ **tablespoons cornstarch**
$1^1/2$ **tablespoons water**

Cut chicken into small cubes. Toss together with beaten egg, white pepper, and 1 teaspoon cornstarch. Set aside for 30 minutes to marinate.

Add 2 tablespoons of oil to wok and tilt to distribute over pan surface. Heat wok to 350 F. Add chicken and stir fry until a little more than half cooked; add onions, carrots and peas and continue stirring until mixture is nearly cooked. Remove chicken and vegetables from wok with a slotted spoon and drain on paper towels. Discard oil in wok and return to heat.

Add 1 tablespoon oil to wok. Return chicken to wok and stir in soy sauce, sherry, sugar and chicken broth; dissolve cornstarch in water and stir into sauce.

Stir-fry until chicken is fully cooked. Serve immediately.

Makes 2 servings.

Test kitchen note: At Epcot Center the experienced Chinese chefs add the 2 tablespoons of oil to a wok that is preheated to 350 F. We altered the recipe for the home cook because splattering of the oil on a very hot surface may be dangerous to a cook inexperienced in working with a wok.

This is one of the popular seafood restaurant's signature items. Serve it with a salad of fresh greens and a crisp, white wine.

Straub's Fine Seafood's Shrimp Scampi
Altamonte Springs, Orlando

1 cup melted butter
1/2 teaspoon white pepper
Salt to taste
2 teaspoons garlic powder
3 tablespoons plus 1 teaspoon
  good-quality sherry (not
  cooking sherry)
2 tablespoons plus 1 teaspoon
  red-wine vinegar
40 large (26- to 30-count)
  shrimp, cleaned and deveined
4 teaspoons flour
2 teaspoons chopped chives

Preheat oven to 450 F.

Mix together butter, white pepper, salt and garlic powder; set aside.

In another bowl, mix sherry and vinegar; set aside.

Place 10 shrimp in each of 4 individual serving-size casserole dishes. Sprinkle each with 1 teaspoon flour and 1/2 teaspoon chopped chives.

Spoon 4 tablespoons of the butter mixture on top of each casserole preparation.

Place casseroles in preheated oven for 4 to 5 minutes. Remove from oven, stir in 1 tablespoon sherry mixture in each casserole. The preparation will thicken slightly. Return to oven and bake for another 4 to 5 minutes. Remove from oven and serve immediately.

Makes 4 servings.

Sweetbreads are the thymus glands of veal, young beef, lamb and pork. When buying, choose sweetbreads that are white (they become red as the animal ages).

Le Coq au Vin's Calf Sweetbreads a l'Orange
Orlando

2 large (about 1¼ pounds)
   sweetbreads
Salt and pepper and flour
½ stick margarine, melted
8 large mushrooms, sliced
1 teaspoon green peppercorns
1 tablespoon finely chopped
   shallots
4 tablespoons dry white wine
1 cup Knorr-Swiss demi-glace
   sauce
½ cup heavy cream
1 orange, cut in 12 half-inch
   slices

Select very white sweetbreads and soak overnight in fresh water, changing water at least twice.

Place sweetbreads in a saucepan with cold water to cover. Bring to boil, reduce heat to simmer and cook gently for 10 minutes. Remove sweetbreads and plunge them into a bowl of cold water to stop cooking process.

When cool enough to handle, trim sweetbreads by cutting away all cartilage and connective tissue.

Cut sweetbreads into 1½-inch-thick slices. Pat dry with towel. Season to taste and dredge in flour. Put melted margarine in a 9-inch-by-9-inch, non-stick baking pan and heat; add sweetbread slices and toss until lightly browned.

Add mushroom slices, peppercorns and shallots. Cook, tossing gently for 2 minutes. Drain off fat and add wine. Simmer on medium heat for 2 minutes; add demi-glace and cream.

Season to taste and braise in the same pan, covered, 10 to 15 minutes in a 375 F oven.

Arrange 4 slices of orange on the edges of four plates. Place slices of sweetbread in circular arrangement on plates and distribute sauce equally among the servings.

Makes 4 servings.

Serve this Italian casserole with garlic-flavored bread sticks and a glass of dry red wine.

Olive Garden Italian Restaurants' Vegetable Lasagna with Alfredo Sauce
Locations throughout Florida

Lasagna noodles

Alfredo sauce:
$^1/_2$ pound (2 sticks) sweet or salted butter

12 ounces ($1^1/_2$ cups) heavy cream

Freshly ground white pepper to taste

$1^1/_2$ cups freshly grated Parmesan cheese

18 slices mozzarella cheese, reserved for assembling lasagna

Ricotta cheese mix:
16 ounces (1 pint) ricotta cheese

2 ounces ($^1/_4$ cup) grated romano cheese

3 ounces ($^3/_4$ cup) shredded mozzarella cheese

2 tablespoons green onion in $^1/_2$-inch slices

2 teaspoons chopped fresh parsley

$^1/_2$ teaspoon salt

Black pepper to taste

$^1/_4$ teaspoon dry basil

$^1/_4$ teaspoon dry oregano

$1^1/_4$ cups cool Alfredo sauce (see note in instructions for making sauce)

Vegetable mix:
4 cups broccoli florets cut in $^1/_4$-inch pieces

2 cups carrots, sliced $^1/_4$-inch thick, then roughly chopped

4 cups mushrooms in $^1/_4$-inch slices

2 cups red bell peppers, diced

1 cup green bell peppers, diced

1 cup yellow onion, diced

2 cups zucchini in $^1/_4$-inch slices

To make Alfredo sauce, heat water to a boil in the bottom of a double boiler. Add butter, cream and pepper to the top pot and heat until butter is completely melted, then stir in Parmesan cheese until melted and blended. Remove top pot and set aside to cool. Divide the sauce into 2 equal portions. Refrigerate one portion to use later.

To cook lasagna strips, take a 9-by-13-inch baking pan and lay out enough dry lasagna strips to ensure you have enough to make three full layers, with very little overlap on each layer. Remove the dry strips and cook according to package directions; drain. Cook the strips only until barely *al dente*, or tender. If precooked too much, the pasta will be too soft and lose its integrity when assembled lasagna is baked.

To make ricotta cheese mix, combine ricotta cheese, $1/4$ cup grated romano cheese, $3/4$ cup shredded mozzarella cheese, 2 tablespoons green onion, 2 teaspoons chopped fresh parsley, $1/2$ teaspoon salt, black pepper to taste, $1/4$ teaspoon dry basil, $1/4$ teaspoon dry oregano, $1^1/4$ cups cooled Alfredo sauce. Blend thoroughly with a rubber spatula. Set aside at room temperature while vegetables are being prepared.

Wash and drain all ingredients listed for vegetable mix. Peel carrots. Cut vegetables to specified dimensions. If cut too large, they will not cover layers sufficiently. Combine all finished vegetables and mix well.

To assemble lasagna, coat the bottom and walls of 9-inch-by-13-inch baking dish with non-stick cooking spray, butter, margarine or oil.

Lay out cooked lasagna strips (about 4) to cover bottom of the dish. Spread $1^1/4$ cups of ricotta cheese mix evenly over the lasagna strips. Top the ricotta cheese mix with 8 cups of vegetable mix and spread out vegetables evenly.

Lay out 9 of the reserved mozzarella cheese slices to cover the layer of vegetable mix.

Repeat this layering — lasagna strips, ricotta cheese mix, vegetable mix, 9 mozzarella slices. Top the second layer of mozzarella cheese slices with lasagna strips and spread them evenly with $1^1/4$ cups of ricotta cheese mix to finish.

Spray a sheet of aluminum foil with cooking spray and cover the baking dish tightly with the foil, sprayed side down. Bake in a 375 F oven for about 1 hour or until the internal temperature of the lasagna is 165 F.

Remove casserole from oven and allow to sit a few minutes, covered, before serving.

Before serving, heat reserved portion of Alfredo sauce and spoon the hot sauce over each slice of lasagna as it is served.

Makes 8 servings.

This Villa Rosa signature dish was first prepared aboard Aristotle Onassis' yacht.

Gus' Villa Rosa's Shrimp a la Onassis
Orlando

12 large raw shrimp, cleaned
and deveined
1 tablespoon butter
1 tablespoon olive oil
Salt and pepper to taste
1 clove garlic, finely minced
1/2 teaspoon oregano
1 tablespoon chopped parsley
1/2 cup scallions, both white
bulbs and green tops, finely
chopped
1/4 pound feta cheese, cut in
1/2-inch cubes
2 tablespoons marsala or
sherry wine (not cooking
sherry)
1 large fresh tomato, chopped,
or 1/2 cup chopped canned
tomatoes
Rice or pasta

Melt butter with oil; add garlic and simmer — do not brown. Add shrimp, salt and pepper; simmer over low heat until half done; add remaining ingredients and simmer for 2 to 3 minutes — do not overcook. Serve over rice or pasta.

Makes 2 servings.

114

Serve this delicious dish with a glass of red zinfandel.

Jordan's Grove's Tri-Color Pasta with Bratwurst and Parmesan and Romano Cream Sauce
Maitland

2 veal sausage bratwurst
8 ounces fresh green, red and
   yellow pasta
2 cups heavy whipping cream,
   divided
1 stick butter
1/4 cup grated Parmesan cheese
1/4 cup grated Romano cheese
Salt and pepper to taste
1/2 tablespoon nutmeg
2 egg yolks

Cook pasta until *al dente*. (For more flavor, cook in chicken stock instead of water.) Drain pasta and set aside.

In a saute pan, brown bratwurst; set aside.

In a saucepan melt butter, add 1 cup of cream. Cook, stirring, until mixture bubbles. Remove pan from heat.

In a bowl, mix egg yolks, cheeses and remainder of cream.

Add egg yolk mixture to heated butter and cream mixture. Stir to mix.

Return preparation to heat until sauce bubbles, slice bratwurst and mix into sauce. Add salt and pepper to taste and about 1/2 tablespoon of nutmeg. Cook until bratwurst is warm.

Reheat pasta by dipping it into hot water. Drain warmed pasta and combine with sauce mixture.

Makes 2 servings.

This classic French vegetable strudel was created by chef Louis Perrotte.

Le Coq Au Vin's Feuillete of Vegetable
Orlando

1 bunch broccoli
1/2 head cauliflower
2 carrots, diced
1 large onion, diced
2 cloves garlic, finely chopped
2 tablespoons butter
3 eggs
2 teaspoons chopped parsley
1 1/2 teaspoons dried basil
1 teaspoon chopped tarragon
Salt and pepper to taste
1 pound Cheddar cheese,
   grated
14 sheets phyllo dough
1/4 cup butter, melted
3 tablespoons sesame seeds
   (optional)
Cheese sauce of choice

Preheat oven to 375 F.

Remove florets from broccoli and cauliflower. Chop stems and core. Steam florets, chopped stems and core with diced carrots until crisp-tender; set aside.

Saute onion and garlic in butter until limp but not browned. In large bowl, beat eggs, add herbs and seasonings. Add grated cheese, sauteed onion mixture and steamed vegetables. Mix well, using care to avoid softening vegetables.

With pastry brush, carefully butter all but one sheet of phyllo dough, placing one on top of the other. Arrange vegetable filling lengthwise in center of dough, leaving about 3 inches on each side. Overlap dough and seal. Place on an oiled baking sheet, folded side down. Butter top of strudel. Sprinkle with sesame seeds, if desired.

Bake for 20 to 30 minutes.

Remove from oven and slice into 10 portions. Cover with warm cheese sauce of your choice and serve immediately.

Makes 10 servings.

La Normandie is a showcase for fine French cuisine. Recipes like this have made it a popular dining spot for years.

La Normandie's Saumon en Croute
Orlando

4 whole fresh spinach leaves,
  cleaned
1 cup boiling water
1 pint fresh whipping cream
14 ounces fresh mushrooms,
  sliced
1 stick butter
1 shallot, chopped
3¼ pounds puff pastry dough,
  fresh or frozen
8 (6-ounce) boneless salmon
  fillets
2 eggs, beaten, for egg wash

Sauce:
1 shallot, chopped
4 tablespoons fresh whipping
  cream
1 pint white wine
2 sticks butter
Salt and pepper to taste

Preheat oven to 400 F.

Add spinach leaves to boiling water. When water returns to boil, remove spinach and squeeze dry.

In a saucepan, cook cream over medium heat until it thickens, about 5 minutes. Place spinach and cream in food processor bowl and process until spinach is pureed. Set spinach and cream mixture aside to cool.

Saute sliced mushrooms and shallot in butter until juice extracted from mushrooms has evaporated. Let vegetables cool.

Roll puff pastry into very thin 6-inch-by-4-inch sheets to make 8 shells.

In the middle of each pastry place 2 tablespoons creamed spinach, 8 sauteed sliced mushrooms, a salmon fillet and salt and pepper to taste.

Fold each corner of the pastry to the center and seal with touch of water.

Place each filled pastry, fold side down, on a lightly greased baking sheet.

Brush each pastry with egg wash. Bake for 35 minutes.

While pastry is baking, prepare sauce. In a saucepan, combine shallot and white wine; cook until liquid has evaporated. Add cream slowly over low heat. Whip in butter.

Remove pastry from oven.

Make horizontal slit in center of each pastry and spoon equal amounts of sauce into each slit. Serve immediately.

Makes 8 servings.

In this preparation, snapper is pan-browned, baked and dressed with a light pine nut-mushroom butter that enhances the delicate flavor of the fish.

Gus' Villa Rosa's Red Snapper with Sauteed Pine Nuts and Mushrooms
Orlando

4 (6- to 8-ounce) snapper fillets
Salt and pepper to taste
Flour
1 egg whipped with
    1 tablespoon water
Butter or salad oil
4 tablespoons pine nuts
2 cups sliced fresh mushrooms
2 tablespoons Madeira,
    marsala or cream sherry
Juice of 1 lemon
1 tablespoon chopped fresh
    parsley

Preheat oven to 350 F.

Season fillets lightly with salt and pepper.

Dip both sides of fillets in flour, shake off excess, dip in egg mixture and drain.

Heat butter or salad oil in a large skillet. Pan-fry fillets golden brown on both sides. Remove fish from heat.

Bake fillets for 5 to 10 minutes, depending on thickness, until fish flakes when touched with a fork.

In a second skillet, saute pine nuts until lightly browned in 2 tablespoons butter. Add mushrooms and saute about 4 to 5 minutes. Add Madeira, lemon juice and chopped parsley. Continue cooking for 1 minute over medium heat. Pour mushrooms, pine nuts and pan juices over baked snapper fillets and serve.

Makes 4 servings.

When preparing this dish, be careful not to overcook the seafood; it can toughen quickly when subjected to too much heat.

Hollywood Brown Derby's Tri-color Pasta with Scallops and Shrimp
Disney-MGM Studios Theme Park, Lake Buena Vista

6 ounces fresh tri-color
   linguine
2 ounces clarified butter
1 medium onion, minced
5 ounces (36- to 40-count)
   shrimp, peeled, deveined
   and tail removed
5 ounces frozen sea scallops
3 ounces feta cheese or to taste
Salt and white pepper to taste
¼ cup half-and-half
5 sprigs parsley, chopped
2 garlic bread sticks, cut in
   half lengthwise

Cream sauce:
2 tablespoons butter or
   margarine
2 tablespoons flour
Salt and white pepper to taste
1 cup milk

To make cream sauce, melt 2 tablespoons of butter in small saucepan over low heat; blend in 2 tablespoons of flour and salt and pepper. Cook over low heat, stirring until smooth and bubbling; remove from heat and stir in 1 cup of milk. Heat just to boiling point, stirring constantly. Cook, stirring, for 1 minute or until thickened.

Set sauce aside and keep warm.

Cook pasta, drain and set aside.

In a skillet, add clarified butter and heat. Stir in minced onions and seafood and saute just until seafood is tender.

Blanch cooked pasta in hot water to reheat and add to saute pan.

Stir in cream sauce and feta cheese.

Adjust seasonings and consistency; if sauce is too thick, stir in half-and-half and reduce to desired consistency.

Divide contents of pan between two serving plates. Garnish with chopped parsley and accompany with a bread stick.

Makes 2 servings.

Chef Tony Pace created this pasta dish that includes lemon-flavored chicken.

Pebbles' Chicken Vesuvio
Longwood, Winter Park, Orlando, Lake Buena Vista

8 tablespoons (1 stick)
  unsalted butter
2 teaspoons capers
2$\frac{1}{2}$ teaspoons chopped garlic
2 teaspoons lemon juice
$\frac{1}{2}$ teaspoon rosemary
$\frac{1}{2}$ teaspoon oregano
$\frac{1}{2}$ teaspoon chopped parsley
$\frac{1}{2}$ teaspoon pepper
$\frac{1}{2}$ teaspoon Tabasco sauce
8 ounces chicken breast,
  skinned and cut into strips
4 ounces demi-glace
2 ounces white wine
1 ounce lemon juice
2 egg yolks
8 ounces perciatelli pasta (very
  thick noodles), cooked and
  drained
4 Italian plum tomatoes,
  heated and kept warm
Chopped parsley for garnish
10 to 12 snow pea pods,
  blanched for garnish
$\frac{1}{2}$ red pepper, julienned for
  garnish
$\frac{1}{4}$ cup grated Romano cheese

In a large saute pan, melt 4 tablespoons of the butter. Add capers, $\frac{1}{2}$ teaspoon of the chopped garlic, lemon juice, rosemary, oregano, parsley, pepper and Tabasco sauce; stir to make Vesuvio butter.

Add chicken strips to pan and saute over medium heat until browned on both sides. Add remaining 2 teaspoons chopped garlic, demi-glace, wine and lemon juice; let mixture cook until reduced in volume by a third. Whisk in remaining 4 tablespoons butter.

Remove pan from heat. Stir in egg yolks and continue stirring until sauce thickens. Add hot pasta and plum tomatoes.

Put pasta on a serving platter. Garnish with parsley, snow peas and red pepper if desired. Top with Romano cheese.

Makes 2 servings.

This dish would make a festive entree for a holiday buffet.

Le Coq au Vin's Shrimp Andre
Orlando

20 (21- to 25-count) shrimp,
  cleaned, split, tail on
1 tablespoon unsalted butter
  to rub on saute pan
2 teaspoons minced garlic
2 teaspoons drained capers
1 tablespoon chopped parsley
½ cup dry white wine
⅓ cup wine vinegar
2 tablespoons minced shallots
½ cup heavy whipping cream
2 sticks unsalted butter
Salt and pepper to taste

Preheat oven to 450 F.

In a small, thick-bottomed saucepan over low heat, reduce by almost half the wine, vinegar and shallots. This may take a little time. The pan ingredients should cook to an almost dry stage.

Stir in whipping cream and again reduce by half over low heat. Add 2 sticks butter in small amounts, whisking constantly; do not allow mixture to boil. Add salt and pepper to taste. Put mixture in a double boiler to keep warm.

Butter 12-inch saute pan and rub garlic all over bottom of pan. Add shrimp to pan and place in oven until they turn pink, not more than 2 minutes.

Remove pan from oven and place on top burner on medium low heat. Pour sauce from double boiler over shrimp and simmer gently for about 1 minute. Drop capers and parsley in pan, stir gently and serve.

Makes 4 servings.

Roasted red peppers and mushrooms add an earthy flavor to this Italian veal dish.

Lido's Italian Restaurant's Veal Sorrento
Orlando

3 medium-size veal
  medallions
Flour
2 tablespoons butter, divided
1 tablespoon olive oil
1 ounce sherry wine (not
  cooking sherry), warmed
$\frac{1}{3}$ cup Italian salad dressing
Pinch dried oregano
Pinch black pepper
Pinch salt
2 artichoke hearts, halved
2 tablespoons sliced
  mushrooms
$\frac{1}{2}$ roasted red bell pepper, cut
  into strips
Grated Romano cheese

Pound medallions lightly between two sheets of waxed paper. Dredge in flour and shake off excess.

Melt 1 tablespoon of butter in a skillet with olive oil. Add veal medallions and saute until lightly browned on each side. Remove veal from pan and reserve.

Add another tablespoon of butter to skillet and melt.

Add sherry and carefully flambe by igniting contents of pan with a long, tapered match.

Stir in Italian salad dressing, oregano, pepper and salt. Return veal to pan; bring to a simmer.

Add artichoke hearts and mushrooms. Lay strips of roasted red pepper over veal pieces and sprinkle with Romano cheese. Cover pan, remove from heat and let steam for 3 minutes to allow flavors to blend.

Makes 1 serving.

This sauce freezes well. Store in an airtight container for up to three months.

Lee's II Family Restaurant's Barbecue Sauce
Eatonville

1 (15-ounce) can tomato sauce
¼ cup Kraft Onion Salad
  Dressing Mix
¼ cup white vinegar
¼ cup dark molasses
2 tablespoons vegetable oil
1 teaspoon dry mustard
1½ cups water
2 tablespoons Worcestershire
  sauce
1 tablespoon chopped
  jalapeno pepper, optional

In a large saucepan, mix all ingredients.

Bring mixture to a rapid boil, reduce heat and simmer 30 to 45 minutes.

Remove from heat and serve.

Makes about 4½ cups sauce.

Test kitchen note: At Lee's II, the ribs are washed, then placed unseasoned on a grill 4 inches from hot coals for about 30 minutes, and turned every 5 to 6 minutes. The slab is then cut in half and placed in a vented, covered dish and microwaved on high (100 percent) power for 20 minutes (this procedure tenderizes the bone). The ribs are returned to the grill, brushed with barbecue sauce, and turned every couple of minutes until done.

This sauce is also good with chicken or chopped pork.

This zesty chicken presentation is served with coriander-flavored rice.

Bailey's Restaurant's Chicken Poblano
Winter Park

Marinade:
1½ cups fresh grapefruit juice
½ cup fresh orange juice
½ yellow onion, julienned fine
½ red onion, julienned fine
1 fresh cubenelle (waxy
   banana) pepper, seeded,
   julienned
2 poblano chili peppers,
   julienned
1 red bell pepper, julienned
1 jalapeno pepper, finely diced
1 teaspoon chopped garlic
¼ cup olive oil, 3 tablespoons
   reserved for saute
⅛ cup or less to taste, coarsely
   chopped cilantro

Saute ingredients:
3 to 4 deboned skinless
   chicken breasts
3 tablespoons reserved olive oil
½ to ⅔ cup heavy cream
Salt and white pepper to taste
Fresh lime juice

Mix marinade ingredients.

Immerse chicken breasts in marinade; put in refrigerator for 4 to 6 hours or overnight.

Remove chicken from marinade and reserve marinade.

Saute chicken in olive oil over medium heat until about two-thirds done.

Stir in ½ to ⅔ cup of marinade, scrape pan to de-glaze.

Reduce marinade by half until it is thick and gelatinous.

Slowly stir in heavy cream, reduce until sauce coats back of spoon. Add salt and white pepper to taste and a squeeze of fresh lime juice.

Remove julienned vegetables with a slotted spoon and reserve for use as garnish.

Serve chicken breasts with sauce over Coriander Rice (recipe follows).

Garnish chicken with reserved julienned vegetables.

Makes 4 servings.

Coriander Rice

4 portions hot cooked rice
1 teaspoon fresh thyme
½ tablespoon ground
  coriander
¼ tablespoon ground cumin
Pinch of cayenne
3 tablespoons butter

Stir all seasonings except butter into hot rice. Add butter and toss ingredients to coat.

Makes 4 servings.

Freeze some of this sauce to have on hand for summer barbeques. It's also delicious brushed on shrimp.

Cheyenne Saloon and Opera House's Barbecue Sauce
Church Street Station, Orlando

32 ounces Heinz 57 Sauce
12 ounces tomato sauce
½ cup cider vinegar
½ cup Worcestershire sauce
½ cup maple syrup or honey
2 tablespoons brown mustard
2 tablespoons horseradish
  sauce
1 teaspoon Tabasco sauce

Blend all ingredients. Refrigerate until needed.

Use as a basting sauce for beef, pork or chicken.

This savory meat and vegetable pie is a traditional Canadian dish.

Epcot Center's Canada Showcase's Tourtiere
Walt Disney World, Lake Buena Vista

1 medium potato, peeled and
finely diced
2 tablespoons vegetable oil
1 small carrot, finely diced
1 small onion, finely diced
1 rib celery, finely diced
1 clove garlic, finely minced
1 pound lean ground pork
Dash sage
Dash ground cloves
Pastry for a 9-inch double-
crust pie

Blanch diced potatoes quickly in boiling water; potatoes should remain firm. Set aside.

Heat oil in heavy skillet, add onions and saute until transparent.

Add carrots, celery and garlic; saute for 3 to 4 minutes.

Add ground pork and saute rapidly over high heat; add spices and blend well.

Set skillet aside to cool, when cool add potatoes, blend well and adjust seasoning.

Line pie pan with pastry, fill with meat and vegetable mixture and cover with top crust.

Slit crust or press with tines of fork to allow steam to escape.

Bake in 350 F oven for 30 to 45 minutes or until crust is golden brown.

Makes 6 servings.

This recipe is from a lovely restaurant located on the shore of Lake Fairy in Longwood. Enzo Perlini's pasta with red sauce and veal is a menu classic.

Enzo's Sugo di Vitello (Red Sauce with Veal)
Longwood

2 (28-ounce) cans Italian pear tomatoes, San Marzano or Progresso with basil, hand-crushed
1/2 cup olive oil, divided
3 cloves garlic, peeled
1/2 cup dry white wine
1/4 pound ground veal
2 small pieces veal bone, meat attached (ask the butcher for veal rib or thigh bone)
Salt and white pepper to taste

Wash bone well and leave it submerged under running water for 30 minutes. Be sure all blood is washed off or it will darken the sauce.

In a medium saucepan put the well-dried bones, garlic cloves and half the olive oil.

When garlic becomes transparent, remove and discard.

Add remaining oil and allow to become hot. Add ground veal; stir and cook well. Add wine.

Scrape bottom of pan with wooden spoon to remove any residue; continue cooking over medium-high heat until wine has evaporated, less than 5 minutes.

Add crushed tomatoes and stir well.

Allow sauce to boil vigorously for several minutes; reduce heat to medium.

After 1 hour, add salt and white pepper to taste.

Remove bones and discard.

If tomatoes have any bitter taste, add some fresh basil but remove it before sauce is served.

Cook 1 to 1 1/2 more hours, or until sauce reaches desired consistency, occasionally stirring gently.

Serve over fresh pasta of choice.

Makes 6 servings.

The Oviedo Inn's chef-owner Ken Kiester stirs in a light roux to add character to the flavorful sauce in this dish.

The Oviedo Inn's Scallops Newburg
Oviedo

2 quarts shrimp or lobster
   stock
2 shallots, finely chopped
2 bunches green onions,
   topped and bulbs finely
   chopped
1/2 pound mushrooms, sliced
2 cups half-and-half
1/3 cup sherry
1 teaspoon thyme
2 to 3 tablespoons olive oil
   or butter
3 pounds medium scallops
1 ounce brandy
Mushroom caps for garnish
Paprika for garnish
Freshly grated Parmesan
   cheese for garnish

Light roux:
1/4 cup flour
1/4 cup butter

To make stock, add 3 to 4 pounds shrimp or lobster shells and mixture of diced vegetables (carrots, onions and celery) to 4 quarts water. Bring to a rapid boil and boil 30 minutes longer to reduce to 2 quarts. Strain.

Prepare a light roux by stirring 1/4 cup flour into 1/4 cup butter over medium heat. Continue stirring until well-blended. Set aside. Bring stock to boil, slowly stir in roux until blended; continue stirring until stock is lightly thickened.

Add chopped shallots, green onions, sherry, mushrooms, thyme, and half-and-half; reduce heat and simmer 15 to 20 minutes.

While sauce is simmering, in separate skillet with 2 to 3 tablespoons olive oil or butter, saute scallops lightly to a golden brown, about 2 to 3 minutes to retain moisture. De-glaze pan with brandy. Place in casserole and cover with finished sauce. Top with mushroom caps, paprika, and grated cheese. Bake, uncovered, 10 minutes in 350 F oven.

Makes 8 servings.

Vegetables &
Side Dishes

A kugel is a baked pudding, usually made with potatoes or noodles. Sweet versions can be served as a side dish or as a dessert.

Meiner's Catering's Noodle Kugel
Orlando

1 pound medium egg noodles
6 large eggs
13 ounces evaporated milk
²/₃ cup sugar, divided
1 cup sour cream
¹/₃ cup golden or seedless raisins
1¹/₂ cups crushed pineapple
1 teaspoon vanilla extract
1¹/₂ cups graham cracker crumbs
¹/₄ cup butter, softened
1 teaspoon cinnamon

Preheat oven to 350 F.

Boil noodles in salt water; drain well. Put noodles in a buttered 8-inch-by-12-inch baking dish.

Beat together eggs, ¹/₂ cup sugar, evaporated milk, sour cream and vanilla.

Sprinkle pineapple and raisins over noodles. Pour egg mixture over entire pan. Use a fork to distribute contents of pan evenly.

Combine graham cracker crumbs, butter, cinnamon and remainder of sugar. Sprinkle over noodle mixture.

Bake for 50 to 60 minutes.

Makes 5 servings.

Au gratin is a French phrase that refers to food that is sprinkled with crumbs and butter or cheese and broiled to form a crisp, golden crust.

Barney's Steak and Seafood's Au Gratin Potatoes
Orlando

½ stick butter
4 tablespoons flour
2¾ cups milk
2 cups shredded Cheddar
  cheese
Dash garlic powder
4 ounces beer
Dash of Worcestershire sauce
Dash of cayenne pepper
Salt and pepper to taste
1 small onion, diced
4 medium potatoes, boiled,
  peeled and diced
Parmesan cheese

Preheat oven to 350 F.

Melt butter in a saucepan. Slowly add flour and blend well. In a separate pot, scald milk. Add scalded milk slowly to butter and flour mixture. When sauce thickens, add Cheddar cheese and garlic.

Blend with wire whisk until cheese is melted and sauce is smooth. Add beer, Worcestershire sauce and cayenne pepper. Blend well and add salt and pepper to taste.

Remove pan from heat.

Saute onions and combine with cheese sauce. Drain potatoes and while potatoes are still hot, add to hot cheese sauce and mix.

Place in a baking pan and top with Parmesan cheese. Place in oven until well-browned.

Makes 6 servings.

This easy side dish can be served as an appetizer as well.

Barney's Steak and Seafood's Marinated Brussels Sprouts
Orlando

3 (10-ounce) packages frozen
   brussels sprouts
1 small onion, chopped
2 cloves fresh garlic, minced
$\frac{1}{4}$ teaspoon thyme
$\frac{1}{4}$ teaspoon oregano
1 teaspoon monosodium
   glutamate (optional)
1 teaspoon chives, chopped
$\frac{1}{3}$ cup sugar
$\frac{1}{2}$ teaspoon salt
$\frac{1}{4}$ teaspoon garlic powder
$\frac{1}{2}$ teaspoon freshly ground
   black pepper
$\frac{1}{4}$ cup tarragon vinegar
$\frac{3}{4}$ cup cider vinegar
$2\frac{1}{2}$ cups salad oil
1 tablespoon dill

Blanche the brussels sprouts briefly in boiling water for no more than 3 minutes, just long enough to thaw the sprouts. Do not let them become soft. The vegetables should be very crisp when marinated. Drain brussels sprouts thoroughly so that the water doesn't dilute the marinade.

Put remaining ingredients in a bowl and mix with a wire whisk.

Combine marinade with brussels sprouts. Refrigerate vegetable mixture in a covered container overnight.

Makes 1 quart.

Shallot paste and a touch of white wine is the winning combination in this crisply textured vegetable medley.

Hemingways' Vegetables du Jour
Hyatt Regency Grand Cypress, Lake Buena Vista

1 cup shallots, peeled
½ cup salad oil
2 to 3 zucchini, cut into
   julienne strips
2 yellow squash, cut into
   julienne strips
2 carrots, cut into julienne
   strips
1 bunch broccoli, florets only
3 tablespoons drawn butter
Salt and pepper to taste
¼ cup white wine
Cherry tomatoes for garnish
Olive oil

In a blender or food processor, mix shallots and salad oil into a paste; set aside.

Blanche carrots and combine with julienned vegetables and broccoli florets.

In a saucepan, heat butter and shallot paste.

Add vegetables and saute briefly. Season to taste with salt and pepper. Add white wine and gently mix ingredients.

Vegetables should be crisp, textured much like a Chinese stir-fry.

Saute cherry tomatoes briefly in a small amount of olive oil and use to garnish servings.

Makes about 15 servings.

Test kitchen note: If cutting back on amount of vegetables prepared, adjust shallot paste used to ½ teaspoon per portion and use just a splash of white wine.

These colorful squash boats are similar in concept to seasoned twice-baked potatoes. They make an attractive addition to the dinner table.

Meiner's Catering's
Baked Stuffed Yellow Squash Boats
Orlando

6 small crookneck yellow
  squash
1 small sweet red pepper or
  pimento, chopped
3 tablespoons butter
3 tablespoons flour
1/2 pint light cream
1 cup frozen green peas
Salt and white pepper to taste
Grated Parmesan cheese

Wash squash.

Trim each squash lengthwise just a tad so that the vegetables can sit without rolling over. On the opposite sides trim off caps by cutting a portion that is little more than 1/4-inch deep. Set caps aside.

Steam or parboil remaining large vegetables until a paring knife indents into skin with minimal resistance. Cool squash.

Hollow out the inside of the vegetables. (A grapefruit knife or melon ball tool can be used to do this.) Remove seeds and discard. Trim stem end to about 1 inch from hollow area.

Line up squash shells in a lightly greased baking pan.

Preheat oven to 375 F.

Finely chop stems and reserved

caps, onion and red pepper. Saute in butter.

Sprinkle flour over mixture and stir to make a roux.

Cook for 1 minute, add cream and continue stirring to make a heavy sauce.

Add green peas, cook another minute and season to taste with salt and white pepper.

Cool mixture, then spoon into squash shells and sprinkle with grated Parmesan cheese.

Bake until cheese is browned and bubbly.

Makes 6 servings.

In its heyday, the Villa Nova was one of Central Florida's most popular restaurants. It closed in early 1990. This simple but elegant side dish was a popular meal accompaniment.

Villa Nova's Stuffed Tomatoes
Winter Park

4 large tomatoes
¹/₂ bunch or 1 large handful spinach, cleaned, blanched and chopped
1 ounce pine nuts, chopped
¹/₂ clove garlic, crushed
1 tablespoon grated Parmesan cheese
1 tablespoon bread crumbs
Salt and pepper to taste
Chopped parsley to taste
Grated Parmesan cheese for garnish

Preheat oven to 350 F.

Cut caps from tomatoes at stem end, scoop out pulp and reserve with trimmed caps. Chop pulp and caps and mix with spinach, pine nuts, garlic and bread crumbs.

Season mixture with salt, pepper and chopped parsley.

If the stuffing mixture is too moist, stir in more bread crumbs.

Stuff tomato shells with mixture and sprinkle with Parmesan. Place in buttered baking pan and bake 15 minutes .

Serve as a garnish or side dish with broiled beef or lamb.

Makes 4 servings.

Plump button mushrooms are perfect for this recipe. Their mild flavor is enhanced by the garlic, onion and pepper seasonings.

Charley's Steak House's Sauteed Mushrooms
Orlando

1 pound whole jumbo
  mushrooms
4 tablespoons butter
4 tablespoons margarine
¼ cup finely chopped onions
¼ teaspoon white pepper
¼ teaspoon granulated garlic
1½ teaspoons beef base

Saute onions in butter, margarine and seasonings until transparent. Add cleaned and trimmed whole mushrooms and let simmer until tender, about 5 minutes.

Makes 5 to 6 servings.

Regulars at Ronnie's know that each meal is accompanied by a bowl of these pickles.

Ronnie's Kosher-Style Pickles
Orlando

Fresh cucumbers, enough to fill 5-gallon crock
3 gallons water
1 pound salt
3 cloves garlic, coarsely chopped
4 ounces mixed pickling spices
1 bunch fresh dill
1 loaf of stale rye bread broken into chunks

Place cucumbers in crock. Mix salt into water and pour over cucumbers. Add garlic, spices and fresh dill on top.

Add rye bread chunks. Cover crock with cheesecloth.

Put a lightweight stone on top of the cucumbers to submerge them in the brine mixture.

Keep crock at room temperature for 3 days. Cure in refrigerator for 5 more days.

Pickles must be stored in refrigerator.

All guests at this cozy Volusia County restaurant are served a bowl of these marinated tomatoes with their meal.

Pondo's Basil Tomatoes
DeLand

4 vine-ripened tomatoes, cut into wedges

Marinade:
2 tablespoons red-wine vinegar
½ cup olive oil
Salt and pepper to taste
1 teaspoon diced fresh garlic
2 tablespoons chopped fresh basil or 1 teaspoon dried basil

Whisk together marinade ingredients, add tomato wedges and marinate 2 hours, covered, at room temperature. Marinade can be reserved, and more tomatoes added for another batch.

Makes 4 servings.

Test kitchen note: If tomatoes are unavailable, substitute lightly steamed green beans.

Pondo's

This is a fool-proof side dish. To determine the quantity of raw grits needed to yield 3⅜ cups cooked, check the proportions given on the package. The amount can vary according to the type of grits used.

Cascade's Cheese Grits Pie
Hyatt Regency Grand Cypress, Lake Buena Vista

3³/₈ cups cooked grits
3 ounces Lorraine Swiss
   Cheese, shredded (available
   at specialty food stores and
   deli counters)
3¹/₂ teaspoons Knorr Swiss
   vegetable broth base
Sprigs of parsley for garnish

Cook grits according to package directions; during the cooking process stir in shredded cheese and vegetable broth base.

With a pastry bag, pipe individual portions onto serving bowls in wedge-shaped fashion. Garnish with parsley sprigs.

Makes 4 servings.

CASCADE

Green beans are available year-round, but the peak season is May through August. Refrigerate uncooked beans, unwashed, in a plastic bag for up to four days.

Garden Terrace's Southern Green Beans
Marriott's Orlando World Center, Lake Buena Vista

2 ounces salt pork
1½ cups tap water
¼ teaspoon ground black
   pepper
2 pounds fresh green beans,
   cleaned, trimmed and sliced
½ cup mineral water

Trim rind from salt pork and dice into ½-inch pieces.

Place diced salt pork in a large pot with tap water and pepper. Cook covered for 30 minutes over medium heat or until salt pork is tender. Add green beans and mineral water. Continue to cook, covered, until beans are crisp-tender. Drain and keep hot until served.

Makes about 10 servings.

This savory side dish is ready in minutes. Serve it with roast chicken or pork.

La Normandie's Sauteed Cucumbers
Orlando

1 stick butter
$1/2$ teaspoon minced garlic
$1/2$ teaspoon chopped shallots
$1/2$ teaspoon chopped parsley
Pinch salt
Pinch white pepper
3 cucumbers, peeled and
   seeded
3 tomatoes, peeled, seeded and
   chopped

Halve cucumbers lengthwise and scoop out seeds.

Cut in 2-inch-by-$1/2$-inch strips; set aside.

Peel, seed and chop tomatoes; set aside.

In large saute pan, melt butter over medium heat; do not allow to scorch. Stir in garlic, shallots, parsley, salt and pepper. Saute mixture lightly.

Stir in tomatoes and julienned cucumber. Saute until cucumbers are tender, about 2 to 3 minutes.

Makes 6 servings.

La Normandie

The Rowena is long gone, but for years it was a downtown Orlando dining favorite. The fare was simple home cooking. Each dish was elegantly presented by the friendly staff.

The Rowena's Lima Bean Casserole
Orlando

1 (10-ounce) box frozen lima
 beans
2 tablespoons minced onions
½ teaspoon salt
¼ teaspoon Beau Monde
 seasoning
1 (10¾-ounce) can cream of
 chicken soup

Preheat oven to 325 F.

Put frozen beans in a small casserole.

Sprinkle with onions and seasonings.

Cover with undiluted soup and bake covered about an hour.

Makes 3 to 4 servings.

Test kitchen note: This recipe is included in an out-of-print collection of The Rowena's recipes. The directions called for preheating the oven to 325 F to 350 F. If your oven tends to have hot spots, preheat the oven to 325 F. If your oven can maintain an accurate temperature of 350 F, preheat it to 350 F.

Breads &
Breakfast Foods

This sweet, spice bread can be served with a dollop of freshly whipped cream as a dessert or served plain with savory pork chops for a sweet side dish.

Townsend's Plantation's Gingerbread
Apopka

2 cups sifted all-purpose flour
2 teaspoons baking soda
1/2 teaspoon salt
2 teaspoons ground ginger
1 1/2 teaspoons ground cinnamon
1/2 teaspoon ground cloves
1/2 teaspoon ground nutmeg
1/2 cup butter or margarine
1/2 cup packed brown sugar
2 eggs
1/2 cup dark molasses
1/2 cup boiling water

In a large bowl, sift together all-purpose flour, baking soda, salt, ground ginger, ground cinnamon, ground cloves and ground nutmeg; set aside.

In another bowl, cream butter or margarine and add sugar and eggs; beat mixture thoroughly.

Add butter mixture to dry mixture and blend thoroughly.

In a small bowl, mix water and molasses.

Add water and molasses mixture to gingerbread mixture. The batter will be thin.

Pour into an 11-inch-by-8-inch greased, paper-lined pan and bake in 325 F oven for about 40 to 50 minutes or until a toothpick inserted in the center comes out clean.

Allow the gingerbread to remain in pan for 5 minutes after removing from oven; cool on a wire rack.

Makes 12 servings.

Serve this bread with sweet butter and mint tea for an afternoon snack. Or, cover with plastic wrap and add a gingham bow to give as a house-warming gift to the new neighbors.

Sleepy Hollow Tea Room's Banana Nut Bread
Orlando

2 cups sifted all-purpose flour
1 teaspoon baking soda
$1^{1}/_{3}$ cups sugar
$^{1}/_{2}$ cup sour milk
2 eggs
$^{1}/_{2}$ cup coarsely chopped
    pecans
1 teaspoon baking powder
$^{3}/_{4}$ teaspoon salt
$^{1}/_{2}$ cup shortening
1 cup mashed banana
1 teaspoon vanilla
1 cup raisins

Preheat oven to 350 F.

Place all ingredients in large mixing bowl; blend. Beat 1 to 2 minutes to reach desired consistency.

Lightly grease a large 9-inch-by-5-inch-by-3-inch loaf pan and 12 medium muffin cups. Fill loaf pan half full and fill muffin tins.

Bake muffins for 10 to 15 minutes in preheated oven. Bake loaf at same temperature for 40 minutes or until a wooden pick inserted near the center comes out clean.

Makes 1 large loaf and 12 muffins or 24 servings.

Sleepy Hollow
Gifts & Tea Room

Add slices of this savory loaf to a holiday buffet table or use to make flavorful chicken and turkey sandwiches.

Nannie Lee's Strawberry Mansion's Pepper Cheese Bread
Melbourne

2 tablespoons oil
2 tablespoons honey or sugar
1 tablespoon black pepper
½ teaspoon basil
1 cup warm water
1 tablespoon or 1 package dry yeast
½ cup warm water
Pinch of salt
3 cups white flour
1 teaspoon salt or more to taste
½ cup grated Cheddar or Romano cheese

In a large bowl, mix oil, honey or sugar, pepper, basil and cup of warm water.

In another bowl, mix dry yeast, ½ cup warm water and pinch of salt. Let yeast mixture sit until bubbles form on top. Add yeast mixture to contents of large bowl.

Gradually stir in flour, 1 teaspoon of salt and cheese. Mix ingredients, adding more flour if necessary, until a firm, elastic dough forms.

Remove dough from bowl and place on a floured surface. Knead dough and add more flour if necessary.

Place dough in an oiled bowl and let rise until double in bulk. Punch down dough. Knead dough a few more times.

Shape dough into a loaf and place in a greased 9-inch bread pan.

Let dough rise until doubled.

Preheat oven to 325 F. Bake bread for 45 minutes to 1 hour.

Makes 1 loaf.

Sweet corn from Zellwood, Fla., is perfect for this recipe. For a fiery variation add some chopped jalapeno peppers to the batter.

Pioneer Hall's Corn Bread
Fort Wilderness, Walt Disney World, Lake Buena Vista

2 cups milk
1 cup vegetable oil
5 eggs
1⅓ cups cornmeal
1¾ cups sugar
1 tablespoon salt
⅛ cup baking powder
3½ cups all-purpose flour
3 cups whole kernel corn,
 fresh or frozen

Preheat oven to 350 F.

If using fresh corn kernels, blanch 1 minute in boiling water and drain; cool corn immediately.

If using frozen corn, rinse corn in hot water and drain.

In a large bowl, combine milk, oil and eggs; whip together thoroughly.

In another bowl, combine cornmeal, sugar, salt, baking powder and flour. Add mixture to liquid mixture and blend until lumps are dissolved and the batter is smooth.

Mix in corn.

Pour batter into a greased 12-inch-by-18-inch pan and bake for about 20 minutes or until bread is golden brown.

Start the day off right with this healthful combination of oats and fruit.

Cascade's Oatmeal with Raisins and Apples
Hyatt Regency Grand Cypress, Lake Buena Vista

1 apple, peeled and chopped
2 cups (1 pint) unsweetened apple juice
1 cup uncooked oatmeal
2 cups skim milk
4 tablespoons raisins
1 tablespoon chopped dates
Dash (slightly less than 1 teaspoon) of vanilla
Pinch of cinnamon
Lemon and orange zest for garnish

Peel and chop apple, cook in apple juice until tender. Stir in skim milk and oatmeal and cook until oatmeal is done, about 15 minutes.

Add cinnamon, vanilla, raisins and dates. Stir and let stand for 5 minutes.

If mixture is too thick, thin by adding apple juice a tablespoon at a time until desired consistency is reached.

If mixture is too thin, cook a little longer.

Garnish with lemon and orange zest.

Makes 5 servings.

The following recipe serves two for breakfast, but you simply can double the amount of bread, bananas, egg, milk and vanilla to make four servings.

Polynesian Village Resort's Stuffed French Toast
Walt Disney World, Lake Buena Vista

2 or 4 slices sourdough bread cut 1-inch thick
1 banana
1/3 cup sugar
1 teaspoon cinnamon
1 egg
1/4 cup milk
1/2 teaspoon vanilla
Oil or shortening for frying
Whipped butter or maple syrup (optional)

Cut a 1-inch pocket in one side of each bread slice.

Cut banana in half crosswise, then split each piece lengthwise. Remove banana peel and stuff 2 pieces of fruit in each pocket of bread; set aside.

Mix sugar and cinnamon; set aside.

Mix egg, milk and vanilla until well-blended.

Heat about 4 inches of oil or shortening in a pan to 350 F.

Dip stuffed bread into egg and milk mixture. Bread slices should soak for a few seconds to let egg mixture penetrate bread.

Fry bread on both sides in hot oil or shortening until lightly browned, about 3 minutes.

Drain bread on paper towels or wire rack.

Sprinkle bread slices with sugar and cinnamon mixture and serve.

If desired, spread with whipped butter and serve with maple syrup.

Makes 2 servings.

Desserts

This decadent dish is worth every calorie.

Pebbles' White Chocolate Bread Pudding with Bittersweet Chocolate and Kahlua Sauce
Longwood, Winter Park, Orlando, Lake Buena Vista

1¹/₂ pounds brioche
¹/₂ pound butter, melted
1 cup milk
3 cups heavy cream
10 egg yolks, beaten
1¹/₂ cups sugar
1 pound imported white
  chocolate
¹/₂ tablespoon vanilla
**Bittersweet Chocolate With
  Kahlua Sauce (recipe
  follows)**

Remove crusts from brioche and discard. Slice rolls into 2-inch cubes and dip in melted butter. Place on baking sheet and toast in 375 F oven until golden brown. Arrange toasted brioche in buttered 2-to-2¹/₂-inch deep baking pan (either 12 or 13 inches square). Bring milk and cream to a boil; remove from heat. Add a little of the hot mixture to beaten egg yolks to bring up their temperature; whisk egg yolks and sugar into milk mixture to make a custard.

Melt chocolate in double boiler, stir into custard, stir in vanilla. Pour over toasted brioche, covering well. With spoon or clean hands work custard into bread. Let stand for 1 hour. Place baking pan in larger pan with hot water coming halfway up sides of pudding to make a water bath. Bake in a 325 F oven for 1 hour. Serve with Bittersweet Chocolate and Kahlua Sauce.

Test kitchen note: Brioche is a French yeast bread. The classic shape has a fluted base and a knotted top. Brioche can be special ordered from most full-service bakeries.

Use only enough cubes to comfortably fill the baking pan.

Bittersweet Chocolate and Kahlua Sauce

½ pound bittersweet
  chocolate
1 cup confectioners' sugar
¼ cup Kahlua
2 tablespoons melted butter

Melt chocolate in double boiler. Fold in balance of ingredients. Serve warm over White Chocolate Bread Pudding.

This is Park Plaza Gardens' interpretation of the French-inspired, vanilla cream-filled meringue called a vacherin.

Park Plaza Gardens' Strawberry Vacherin
Winter Park

6 egg whites at room temperature
¹/₂ teaspoon cream of tartar
2 cups sugar
1¹/₂ teaspoons vanilla
Vanilla ice cream
1 quart whipping cream, whipped
Whole fresh strawberries

Strawberry sauce:
³/₄ pint fresh strawberries
2 tablespoons powdered sugar
Dash of orange liqueur

Beat whites with cream of tartar in clean grease-free mixing bowl at high speed until voluminous (but far from dry). At medium speed, add 1 tablespoon of sugar at a time, slowly. To avoid a gritty meringue, the sugar must be added slowly. When all sugar has been added, stir in vanilla.

Line a baking sheet with parchment paper. With a 16-inch pastry bag and large tip (such as Ateco No. 7 star tip), pipe a 3-inch closed circle, starting in the center and piping out in a spiral. There should be enough batter to make 10 to 12 meringues and an equal number of small rosettes to top each vacherin.

Bake at 150 F to 175 F for about 1 hour and 45 minutes or until meringues are firm and dry.

The meringues will keep nicely for a week if stored covered in a dry place. Do not refrigerate.

To make strawberry sauce, puree ³/₄ pint fresh strawberries with

2 tablespoons powdered sugar and a dash of orange liqueur; set aside.

To assemble dessert, place a scoop of ice cream in center of each meringue. Starting at the bottom of meringue and continuing over top of ice cream, pipe on four wide, vertical ribbons of whipped cream; be lavish in amount of whipped cream used.

Position fresh strawberries on whipped-cream ribbons. Top each meringue with a little meringue rosette cap.

Carefully drizzle with strawberry sauce.

Makes 10 to 12 meringues.

All cheesecakes profit by a thorough chilling before serving. Store covered so that the dessert doesn't absorb other flavors from foods in the refrigerator.

Oviedo Inn's Polly's Cheesecake
Oviedo

Butter to grease pan
¼ cup graham cracker crumbs
2 pounds cream cheese,
   softened to room
   temperature
1¾ cups sugar
4 eggs
⅛ cup heavy cream
1 teaspoon lemon extract

Preheat oven to 300 F.

Butter sides and bottom of metal 8-inch-by-3-inch Wilton (No. 506-1083) cake pan (do not use springform pan). Place graham cracker crumbs inside and shake until coated. Shake out any excess crumbs. Set pan aside.

Place cream cheese in large mixing bowl; beat on medium speed until smooth. Add sugar, eggs, heavy cream and lemon extract; beat until smooth and creamy. Pour into prepared pan and shake gently to level mixture.

Place pan with cake in another larger pan with water ½-inch deep.

Bake 2 hours. Turn oven off and let cake stay in oven for 1 hour (do not open door).

Remove from oven and let cake cool to room temperature. Turn cake upside down on a cake plate. Cut cake into portions with a fine thread or dental floss. Portions may be wrapped tightly with plastic wrap and frozen.

Makes 12 servings.

Test kitchen note: Wilton pans are available in stores that specialize in cake decorating equipment and in some craft stores.

Add this chiffon pie to a Thanksgiving dinner menu for a delicious grand finale.

Lido's Italian Restaurant's Pumpkin Chiffon Pie
Orlando

1 (9-inch) graham cracker pie
   shell
1 envelope unflavored gelatin
¾ cup light brown sugar,
   lightly packed, divided
1½ teaspoons Spice Island
   Pumpkin Pie Spice
¾ cup evaporated milk
3 eggs, separated
1½ cups Libby's canned
   pumpkin
1 container La Creme whipped
   topping
Whipped cream for garnish,
   optional

In medium saucepan, combine contents of 1 envelope of unflavored gelatin, ½ cup brown sugar and pumpkin pie spice.

Stir ¾ cup of evaporated milk and 3 egg yolks into gelatin and brown sugar mixture. Blend ingredients well.

Let egg yolk mixture stand for 1 minute.

Place saucepan over low heat, stir until mixture thickens slightly, about 5 minutes.

Remove saucepan from heat.

Slowly stir in 1½ cups of canned pumpkin.

Chill until mixture mounds slightly when dropped from a spoon.

Beat egg whites in medium bowl until soft peaks form.

Gradually add remaining sugar and beat until stiff.

Fold in pumpkin mixture and La Creme, turn into pie shell and chill until firm.

Garnish with whipped cream, if desired.

Makes 8 servings.

This is a rich custard dotted with fresh berries and topped with a thick round of sugar. Crack the sugar with a spoon and enjoy the crunchy-creamy contrast in texture.

Le Coq au Vin's Creme Brulee
Orlando

16 egg yolks
1 cup sugar
2 cups milk
3 cups whipping cream
2 tablespoons pure vanilla
  extract
½ pound dark brown sugar
Raspberries or strawberries

Preheat oven to 400 F.

In a large mixing bowl, combine egg yolks and sugar. In saucepan, bring milk, cream and vanilla to boil. Stirring constantly, add the hot milk mixture to egg mixture.

Pour this custard into 13 individual 5-ounce white ramekin cups. Place cups in a large, oblong baking pan. Fill with water so that the water level is halfway up the side of the custard cups.

Bake for 30 minutes. Remove ramekins from pan and cool. When cold, sprinkle brown sugar on top, and under very hot broiler, burn sugar. Cool ramekins again.

To serve, spoon out Creme Brulee onto a dessert plate or bowl and serve with raspberries or strawberries.

Makes 13 (5-ounce) servings.

This dessert is a sure-fire hit with peanut butter lovers. Be sure to use smooth peanut butter when making it, not chunky.

Townsend's Fishhouse and Tavern's Peanut Butter Pie
Orlando

1 (9-inch) deep graham cracker
   pie shell
1 cup smooth peanut butter
1 cup sugar
1 cup cream cheese
1 ounce melted butter
1 teaspoon vanilla extract
1 cup heavy whipping cream
1/2 cup semisweet chocolate
5 ounces chopped unsalted
   peanuts
1 tablespoon water

In a large mixing bowl, combine peanut butter, sugar, cream cheese, melted butter and vanilla. Mix thoroughly until smooth and creamy; set mixture aside.

Use mixer to beat whipping cream until soft peaks form. Gradually mix peanut butter mixture into whipped cream; then spoon into pie shell.

Refrigerate pie for 6 hours.

Melt chocolate with water in a double boiler. Spread lightly over pie filling and sprinkle with chopped peanuts.

Refrigerate pie until firm.

Makes 1 (9-inch) pie or 8 servings.

Memories Gourmet Grill closed its doors long ago. Tim Rosendahl, the talented chef behind the popular Volusia County restaurant, now performs his culinary magic at Walt Disney World.

Memories Gourmet Grill's Bailey's Hazelnut Chocolate Mousse
Daytona Beach

12 ounces semisweet chocolate, finely chopped
1 tablespoon pure vanilla extract
6 jumbo egg yolks
4 ounces Bailey's Irish Cream liqueur
4 ounces hazelnuts, roasted, peeled and coarsely chopped (about 1/3 cup)
1 quart pasteurized heavy cream
Chocolate shavings for garnish
Fresh raspberries for garnish
Whipped cream for garnish
Chopped hazelnuts for garnish

Melt chocolate and vanilla together in a double boiler over low heat.

Whip egg yolks on high speed with wire attachment for 5 minutes. Turn mixer to a slower speed and add chocolate mixture; slowly add Bailey's Irish Cream.

Remove from bowl and put into a larger bowl.

Without washing the first bowl add cream and whip until stiff but not dry. Fold cream into chocolate mixture along with hazelnuts. Refrigerate overnight to firm up. (More or less cream may be added depending on how rich you want the dessert to be.)

Garnish with a small amount of chocolate shavings, fresh raspberries, whipped cream or chopped hazelnuts.

This is a lightly tart and refreshing dessert. Serve it garnished with fresh mint or sugared lemon twists.

Straub's Fine Seafood's Lemon Mousse
Altamonte Springs, Orlando

½ cup lemon juice
½ cup sugar
4 egg yolks, beaten
2 teaspoons grated lemon rind
2 cups whipping cream

Heat lemon juice, sugar, egg yolks and lemon rind over medium heat. Do not allow mixture to boil. Cook and stir until thickened, about 5 minutes; cool mixture.

Whip cream until stiff peaks form; gently fold into cooled lemon mixture. Pour mousse into individual serving dishes; chill for a few hours before serving.

Makes 8 servings.

The combination of white chocolate and dark chocolate wafers makes a wonderful presentation for a special-occasion dinner.

Pebbles' White Chocolate Mousse
Longwood, Winter Park, Orlando, Lake Buena Vista

1/2 **pound French or Swiss imported white chocolate**
1 pint whipping cream
1/4 **cup confectioners' sugar**
5 eggs, separated
2 tablespoons hazelnut liqueur
1/4 **cup sugar**
Pinch of cream of tartar
Thin dark chocolate wafers (available in specialty shops) and chocolate wafer sprinkles for garnish

Melt white chocolate in double boiler until smooth; set aside.

Whip cream, gradually adding powdered sugar, until firm and fluffy. Reserve mixture in the refrigerator.

Separate eggs, carefully keeping whites as clean as possible. Place yolks in bowl and whisk in liqueur.

In another bowl, add egg whites that have warmed to room temperature and cream of tartar. Whip egg whites, gradually adding sugar, until soft peaks form.

Mix warm melted chocolate with egg yolk mixture. Fold in whipped cream. Gently fold in whipped egg whites. Divide mixture among 12 wine glasses. Cover each glass snugly with plastic wrap and refrigerate overnight.

At serving time, remove from refrigerator, discard plastic wrap and garnish portions with whole chocolate wafers and wafer crumbs.

Makes 12 servings.

This easy-to-make cobbler is just the thing for tailgate parties or afternoon picnics.

Crown Hotel's Blueberry-Apple Cobbler
Inverness

4 cups canned sliced apples
2 cups blueberry pie filling
1¼ cups all-purpose flour
2 sticks butter or margarine
1½ cups sugar
⅛ tablespoon cinnamon
Whipped cream or vanilla ice cream for garnish

Preheat oven to 350 F.

Mix together apples and blueberry filling and spread on bottom of 9-inch-by-13-inch casserole dish.

Place flour in mixing bowl and add butter cut into small pieces; rub flour and butter together with fingers until mixture is of bread crumb consistency.

Blend in sugar and cinnamon. Sprinkle mixture over apple and blueberry base.

Bake for 45 to 50 minutes or until golden brown. Serve warm with whipped cream or vanilla ice cream.

Makes 12 large servings.

Test kitchen note: Phyllis Gray of *The Orlando Sentinel* test kitchen staff found this to be a very rich dessert. The top crust bakes to a soft, crumbly consistency. Gray said a larger pan can be used to make this recipe, if desired.

The Crown Hotel

This is a traditional Norwegian dessert that is the highlight of the annual Christmas Eve dinner.

Akershus Restaurant's Rice Cream
Norway Showcase, Epcot Center, Walt Disney World

1 pound small grain white
  rice, not instant
3 cups water
4 cups milk
1 teaspoon salt
2 cups heavy cream
4 tablespoons sugar
2 teaspoons vanilla extract
Strawberry Sauce (recipe
  follows)

Cook rice with water and salt for 15 minutes, covered. Add milk and cook 30 more minutes or until rice is tender and mixture is thick. Chill rice in refrigerator.

Whip cream with sugar and vanilla. Gently fold whipped cream into chilled rice. Serve with Strawberry Sauce.

Makes 10 (8-ounce) servings.

Strawberry Sauce

2 cups strawberry preserves
1 cup water
1 tablespoon lemon juice

Place all ingredients in blender or food processor. Mix until blended.

Serve with Rice Cream or ice cream.

Makes 10 servings.

Whipped egg whites form the base of this flourless cake. Serve slices in a pool of vanilla sauce.

Omni International Hotel's Flourless Chocolate Cake
Orlando

5 squares semisweet chocolate
5 egg yolks
5 egg whites
¾ cup sugar
¾ stick of butter, melted
Icing (recipe follows)
Vanilla Sauce (recipe follows)

Whip sugar and egg whites to make meringue.

Melt chocolate in double boiler; fold chocolate and egg yolks together. Fold into meringue; then fold in melted butter. Spoon into 9-inch springform pan and bake in 350 F oven for 1 hour and 15 minutes or until tested done. Cool on rack, remove from pan and frost with icing.

Icing:

1 cup heavy cream
8 ounces semi-sweet chocolate, melted

Beat together until blended and smooth.

Vanilla Sauce:

¼ teaspoon vanilla
4 ounces (½ cup) heavy cream
½ egg yolk

Bring heavy cream to a boil and turn heat off. Stir in egg yolk until thick; then add vanilla. Vanilla Sauce should be poured around each slice of cake as it is served, not on top of the cake.

These slice-and-bake cookies are studded with buttery macadamia nuts and rich chocolate chips. Serve with milk for an after-school snack.

Buena Vista Palace's
Macadamia Chocolate Chip Cookies
Lake Buena Vista

2¹/₂ cups all-purpose flour
1 teaspoon salt
1 teaspoon baking soda
1¹/₂ sticks butter
³/₄ cup light brown sugar
2 cups semisweet milk
  chocolate chips
²/₃ cup confectioners' sugar
1 egg
1 teaspoon vanilla
1 cup chopped macadamia
  nuts
¹/₃ cup chopped pecans

Sift dry ingredients; set aside.

Cream butter and sugars. Blend in egg and vanilla.

Stir in sifted dry ingredients, chopped nuts and chocolate chips.

Roll dough into the shape of fat cylinder. Refrigerate dough for 1 hour.

Preheat oven to 325 F.

Slice dough and place on a cookie sheet.

Bake for about 10 minutes. Remove cookies from pan and let cool on wire racks.

Makes about 1 dozen cookies depending on diameter desired.

This key lime pie variation uses no egg yolks. It is a cool, refreshing dessert that firms up in the freezer until ready to serve.

Aunt Catfish's Key Lime Pie
Port Orange

2 (14-ounce) cans Eagle Brand
  condensed (not evaporated)
  milk
½ cup key lime juice
1 (9-inch) graham cracker
  crumb crust, baked
Whipped cream

Combine condensed milk and key lime juice. Pour mixture into pie shell. Put pie in freezer until shortly before serving time.

Remove pie from freezer to soften slightly and top with freshly whipped cream.

Makes 1 (9-inch) pie.

The Magic Shell product called for in this recipe can be found in the cake decorating or the ice cream topping sections of most supermarkets.

Capt. Appleby's Inn's Boat Sinker Pie
Mount Dora

2 tablespoons butter
3 (1-ounce) squares
   unsweetened chocolate
4 eggs
3 tablespoons light Karo syrup
1½ cups sugar
¼ teaspoon salt
1 teaspoon vanilla extract
1 (9-inch) pie shell, unbaked
Coffee-flavored ice cream
Chocolate Magic Shell
Whipped cream
Stemmed cherries for garnish

Preheat oven to 325 F.

Melt butter and chocolate in top of double boiler. Cool mixture slightly.

Whip eggs, Karo syrup, sugar, salt and vanilla in mixing bowl on high speed until light. Add chocolate mixture to egg mixture. Mix thoroughly and pour into an unbaked pie shell.

Bake 25 minutes. Increase temperature to 350 F and bake 5 minutes longer or until crusty on top.

Cool pie and place in freezer.

To serve, remove pie from freezer and allow to partially thaw. Top each piece with a scoop of ice cream and pour Magic Shell over entire dessert.

Top with whipped cream and garnish with a stemmed cherry.

Serve while still slightly frozen.

Makes 1 (9-inch) pie or 8 servings.

This is a traditional Kentucky Derby Day dessert. It gets a subtle kick from the bourbon.

The Gables' Run for the Roses Pie
Mount Dora

1 cup granulated sugar
1/2 cup all-purpose flour
1/2 cup butter or margarine, melted and slightly cooled
2 eggs, slightly beaten
2 tablespoons bourbon
1 teaspoon vanilla extract
1 cup semisweet chocolate morsels
1 cup chopped pecans or walnuts
1 (9- or- 10-inch) pie shell, unbaked

Preheat oven to 325 F.

Combine sugar, flour, butter, eggs, bourbon and vanilla in a mixer bowl; beat until well-blended. Stir in chocolate morsels and nuts. Pour into pie shell.

Bake in preheated oven for 50 minutes to 1 hour or until pie is set and top cracks. Cool pie on a wire rack.

Makes 8 to 10 servings.

This dessert is from Swabia in Germany's Black Forest region. Chocolate curls and cherries adorn the top of this triple-decker treat.

Black Forest Cake
German Showcase, Epcot, Walt Disney World

Cake:
5 eggs
3 egg yolks
2/3 cup sugar
3/4 cup cake flour, sifted
6 tablespoons unsweetened cocoa
1/4 teaspoon baking powder
1/4 teaspoon baking soda
1 1/2 teaspoons vanilla extract

Syrup:
1/3 cup water
1/2 cup sugar
3 tablespoons Kirsch cherry liqueur

Filling and frosting:
1 1/4 cups cherry pie filling
3 tablespoons cherry liqueur
1 pint heavy cream, whipped
12 ounces shaved semisweet chocolate

Preheat oven to 350 F.

Combine eggs, egg yolks and 2/3 cup sugar. Beat until thick and light.

Sift together flour, cocoa, baking powder and baking soda. Gradually fold flour mixture into egg mixture. Fold in vanilla. Pour batter into 3 (8-inch) round cake pans that have been lined with a greased circle of waxed paper. Bake for 18 to 20 minutes until top springs back when pressed.

Cool on rack for 10 minutes.

To make syrup, bring 1/3 cup water and 1/2 cup sugar to a boil. Add 3 tablespoons of liqueur. Cool mixture and set aside.

To make filling and frosting, combine 1 1/4 cups cherry pie filling with 3 tablespoons cherry liqueur; set aside.

Put 1 cake layer on a flat serving plate. Drizzle 1/3 of the syrup mixture onto cake layer. Top with a portion of the pie filling mixture.

Add a second layer, drizzle with $^1/_3$ of the syrup mixture and top with remaining pie filling mixture.

Top with final cake layer. Drizzle with remaining syrup mixture. Frost cake with whipped cream and sprinkle with shaved chocolate.

If desired, decorate cake with remaining cherries from pie filling. Refrigerate cake until ready to serve.

Makes 14 servings.

Use walnuts or pecans for the chopped nuts

Use walnuts or pecans for the chopped nuts called for in this recipe.

The Gables' Mississippi Mud Cake
Mount Dora

2 cups sugar
2 sticks margarine
2 tablespoons cocoa
4 eggs
1 teaspoon vanilla
1½ cups all-purpose flour
1½ cups chopped nuts
1½ cups coconut, optional
1 pint Kraft's marshmallow
  creme

Frosting:
1 pound confectioners' sugar
1 stick butter
½ cup cocoa
½ cup Pet evaporated milk

Preheat oven to 350 F.

Combine sugar, margarine and cocoa. Add eggs and vanilla. Beat ingredients until well-blended.

Add flour, nuts and coconut. Beat mixture well, about 2 minutes.

Pour batter into a greased 9-inch-by-13-inch pan. Bake for 30 to 45 minutes, being careful not to overbake.

Cake will be textured somewhat like a brownie.

Remove cake from oven and cover with marshmallow creme. Let cake cool in pan.

To make frosting, cream 1 pound confectioners' sugar, 1 stick butter, ½ cup cocoa and ½ cup Pet evaporated milk until smooth and fluffy.

Spread on cooled cake.

Makes 16 to 18 servings.

Test kitchen note: Marshmallow creme is a thick, whipped mixture available in jars in grocery stores. It is used in fudge, as an ice cream topping and as a filling for cakes and candies.

This mounded banana cream pie is an easy-to-assemble dessert. Choose firm, just-ripe bananas when buying ingredients for this recipe.

Barney's Steak and Seafood's Banana Cream Pie
Orlando

1 quart heavy whipping cream
1 pint half-and-half
1 (14-ounce) package instant
   vanilla pudding mix
1 cup crushed ice
1 (9-inch) baked pie shell
2 bananas
Whipped cream for garnish
Banana slices for garnish

Put heavy whipping cream and half-and-half in mixing bowl; blend in pudding mix. Whip at lowest speed on electric mixer. Add ice and continue mixing for about five minutes. Increase to medium speed and mix another 5 minutes; turn mixer to high speed and mix until pudding is very stiff.

Line bottom of pie crust with slices from 1 banana.

Fill pie shell with about half the prepared filling until level with top, and top with slices of the second banana.

Pile on the rest of the filling, shaping with rubber spatula to form a high center cone. (This will be a very high pie.) Refrigerate for at least 1 hour until thoroughly chilled.

To serve, top each piece with freshly whipped cream and a few slices of banana for garnish.

Makes 1 (9-inch) pie or 8 servings.

This layered cheesecake gets two extra flavor punches from raspberry and apricot jams.

Le Cellier's German-Style Cheesecake
Canada Showcase, Epcot Center, Walt Disney World

Dough:
$1/4$ cup sugar
2 sticks butter
1 whole egg
4 drops vanilla extract
$2^1/2$ cups all-purpose flour

White Cake:
1 standard-size box plain white cake mix (no pudding added)

Cheese mixture:
$2^1/2$ cups cream cheese
$1/3$ cup sugar
$1/2$ cup milk
1 cup heavy cream
1 tablespoon dissolved gelatin

$1/4$ cup raspberry jam
$1/4$ cup apricot jam
3 tablespoons powdered sugar
1 cup heavy cream, whipped
Sliced almonds for garnish

Preheat oven to 375 F.

Mix dough ingredients, except flour, until smooth. Add flour and chill 30 minutes for easy handling. Roll out dough into a 10-inch round ($1/4$-inch thick). Bake at 375 F for 15 minutes, until golden brown. Cool and spread $1/4$ cup of raspberry jam on top.

Place this layer into a 10-inch springform pan.

Prepare white cake as directed on box. Cool and cut two $1/4$-inch layers off the top. Spread $1/4$ cup of apricot jam on top of one layer and place this layer into the springform pan.

Cream sugar, milk, and cream cheese. Whip the heavy cream and gelatin. Fold into cheese mixture. Fill the springform almost to the top with cheese mixture. Put the other white cake layer on top.

Chill cake for 2 hours.

Remove from pan and sprinkle powdered sugar on top of cheesecake. Spread whipped cream around the sides of the cake and sprinkle the sides with sliced almonds.

Makes 10 servings.

The mild, sweet flavor of pumpkin is a perfect accent for all kinds of desserts, especially cheesecakes.

Sweets Etcetera's Pumpkin Cheesecake
Orlando

2 pounds cream cheese
1½ cups packed dark brown
 sugar
¼ cup flour
1 teaspoon cinnamon
1 teaspoon allspice
¼ teaspoon ginger
1 (16-ounce) can pumpkin
5 eggs

With electric mixer, mix cream cheese, packed brown sugar, flour, cinnamon, allspice, ginger and pumpkin until smooth, scraping down sides of bowl at least once.

With the mixer turned off, add 2 eggs. Turn mixer on medium speed to blend eggs with cream cheese mixture. Add 3 more eggs, one at a time, while the mixer is running. Scrape down the sides of the bowl and mix again.

Pour mixture in a buttered and floured 9-inch springform pan. Bake in a preheated 250 F oven for 2½ hours.

Makes 9 servings.

Dessert souffles can be baked, chilled or frozen and are most often flavored with fruit purees, chocolate or liqueurs.

La Normandie's Souffle Grand Marnier
Orlando

Sugar for dusting bowls

Base:
½ stick unsalted butter, melted
⅔ cup flour
1 pint half-and-half
½ cup sugar
Peel from ½ an orange, grated

Mix:
8 egg yolks
4 ounces Grand Marnier
8 egg whites
⅔ cup sugar

Sauce (recipe follows)

Wipe eight individual-serving souffle bowls to remove any moisture. Dust the inside of the bowls with sugar.

Make roux with butter and flour; set aside.

Bring half-and-half, ½ cup of sugar and orange peel to a boil.

Add roux to half-and-half mixture. Stir until smooth and return to boil. Keep mixture warm.

Separate eggs. In mixing bowl, mix egg yolks, Grand Marnier and half-and-half mixture.

In another mixing bowl, whip egg whites and sugar. When egg whites start to thicken, add to the Grand Marnier mixture. Stir gently with spatula.

Pour into eight sugar-dusted souffle bowls.

Fill a large pan with water ¼ full. Place souffle bowls in pan.

Bake in 350 F oven for 20 minutes. Serve immediately.

Sauce for Souffle Grand Marnier

1 cup milk
¼ cup sugar
1 teaspoon vanilla
3 eggs
1 ounce Grand Marnier

Bring to a boil (be careful not to let it reach beyond the boiling point) milk, sugar and vanilla.

In separate bowl, whip eggs.

Stir eggs carefully into heated liquid. Add Grand Marnier to mixture.

Pour sauce over souffles.

Make 8 servings.

William Higgins, the Peabody's executive sous chef, and Walter Wassmer, executive pastry chef, broke down this recipe to home kitchen proportions for your pleasure. Don't even begin to count the calories. Every bite is worth it.

Dux's Pecan Tart with Honey Ice Cream and Caramel Sauce
The Peabody, Orlando

1¼ cups dark Karo syrup
2 tablespoons sugar
3 tablespoons flour, sifted
3 whole eggs
Pinch of salt
2 drops vanilla extract
2 tablespoons butter, melted
½ cup pecans, chopped
1½ cups pecan halves
Caramel Sauce (recipe
    follows)
Honey Ice Cream (recipe
    follows)

Sugar pie crust:
¼ cup butter, softened
⅜ cup cake flour, sifted
¼ cup powdered sugar
Pinch of salt
2 drops vanilla extract
1 egg yolk

Work all ingredients listed for sugar pie crust into softened ¼ cup of butter with hands, blender with paddle or food processor.

Place in refrigerator on sheet pan to chill well while preparing pecan filling.

In stainless steel bowl of blender, combine syrup and sugar; whip together. Add sifted flour, continuing to blend. Add eggs, one by one, then salt and vanilla extract. Slowly add melted butter, then stop.

Do not whip too much after butter has been added.

Mix in chopped pecans.

Roll out sugar dough.

Line a 9- or 10-inch pie pan or ring with pastry, trim edges.

Spread tart shell with pecan filling, place pecan halves on top to garnish.

Bake in preheated 325 F oven for about 20 minutes or until tart sets up, do not allow it to get too brown.

Filling should be very dense and almost brittle.

Let cool and remove from pan, cut portions with a very sharp knife.

Test kitchen note: It is best served warm with Caramel Sauce and Honey Ice Cream. (Frozen pie shell may be substituted, if desired.)

Caramel Sauce

¼ stick butter
1 scant cup granulated sugar
2 tablespoons corn syrup
½ cup water
¼ cup cream

Combine butter, sugar, corn syrup and water. Boil together over medium heat.

When water has evaporated, the sugar will begin to brown. Remove from heat and stir in cream. Return to low heat and lightly simmer until desired consistency is achieved.

Honey Ice Cream

6 egg yolks
1½ cups sugar
2 cups milk
¾ cup heavy cream
½ cup honey

In blender, combine yolks and sugar. Whip until eggs appear opaque.

Heat milk and cream together. Just before mixture reaches the boiling point slowly add to egg yolk mixture with blender running. Whip for 3 to 5 minutes; add honey. Let mixture cool; then freeze in a stainless steel or plastic container.

This sweet-tart dessert graces the cover of this book. It is a delicious grand finale for a Florida dinner.

Sweets Etcetera's Key Lime Pie
Orlando

1 (14-ounce) can condensed
  milk
3 ounces plain yogurt
5 large egg yolks
5 ounces Key lime juice
Prepared graham cracker crust
Whipped cream (optional)

Preheat oven to 350 F.

Mix all ingredients in a mixer bowl using a whip attachment. Pour into graham cracker crust.

Bake for 10-12 minutes.

Chill pie. Top with whipped cream and serve.

Makes 8 servings.

Test kitchen note: For a dramatic presentation, mix graham cracker crumbs, butter and a small amount of water to make a thick crumb paste. With a wooden ice cream stick, add the paste to the rim of the filled, baked pie. When pie chills, decorative rim will become firm.

The Rowena was a lovely eatery in downtown Orlando. It closed long ago, but readers still request recipes for foods that were served in its gracious dining room.

The Rowena's Chocolate Mint Pie
Orlando

1½ sticks margarine or butter, softened

1½ cups powdered sugar, packed

3 eggs

4 (1-ounce) squares Hershey's or Bakers unsweetened baking chocolate, melted in a double boiler

1 teaspoon McCormick's Pure Mint or Peppermint extract

1 graham cracker pie crust

Vanilla ice cream (optional)

Combine the softened butter with the powdered sugar and cream well. Add eggs, one at a time, blending after each addition.

Add melted chocolate. Add extract and blend mixture.

Pour mixture into a graham cracker crust. Chill for several hours in the refrigerator or freeze. An hour before serving remove from refrigerator.

Serve slices with vanilla ice cream, if desired.

Makes 8 servings.

Glossary

Adjust: When a recipe says to "adjust the seasonings," taste the dish at this stage of preparation. Add salt, spices or herbs, if needed, to balance the flavor.

Al dente: An Italian term for cooking pasta, that translates "to the tooth." It means the food should be soft but still have firmness and bite.

Alla: An Italian word that means "as done by, in, for or with."

Amandine: A French word meaning "garnished with almonds."

Bake: To cook by dry heat in the oven.

Baking sheet: A flat sheet of metal with at least one side turned up for easy handling.

Balsamic vinegar: A type of slightly sweet, smooth-tasting Italian wine vinegar that has been aged in oak barrels. It is not sour like American vinegar and can be used alone on salads or vegetables, or mixed into sauces and dressings. Balsamic vinegar is available in most grocery stores and specialty food markets.

Basil: A member of the mint family that adds a pungent, licorice flavor to food. It is used in Italian, French and American cooking. Use basil fresh or dry. Cook fresh leaves only briefly or use them raw as cooking destroys the flavor.

Beau Monde: A seasoning in the Spice Island line of spices. It is available at most supermarkets.

Bisque: A thick, rich soup usually consisting of pureed seafood and cream.

Blanch: To plunge food into boiling water briefly, then into cold water to stop the cooking process.

Boil: "Bring to a boil" means to heat the liquid mixture until bubbles break the surface. A "full rolling boil" is when the liquid is extremely active and the action is not dissipated by stirring.

Bouillon granules: The granulated form of dehydrated concentrated beef, chicken or vegetable broth.

Braise: A cooking method for meat or fibrous vegetables. Food is first browned in a small amount of oil, then simmered in a small amount of liquid (usually broth, wine or tomatoes) inside a tightly covered casserole. Foods can be braised in an oven or on the stovetop.

Brioche: A type of delicate French yeast roll.

Broil: To cook food under or above the heat source. In an oven, place the food directly under the heat source. On a grill, put food directly over charcoal or other heat source.

Brown rice: The grain in its whole, most nutritious form, before the outer shell of bran is polished away. Brown rice has a chewier texture but takes longer to cook than white, polished rice. It is best in salads, pilafs, casseroles and stews.

Bulgur: Wheat that has been cracked, steamed and dried. It only requires soaking in hot water or broth to prepare. Bulgur has a nutty flavor and chewy texture.

Canola oil: A highly polyunsaturated cooking oil made from rapeseed. One brand is Puritan.

Capers: The unopened flower buds of a caper shrub. The buds are pickled in brine and used to add a faintly sour zing to sauces, salads and dips. The best are the smallest or *nonpareilles* capers.

Cilantro: The fresh leaves of the coriander plant that have a peppery, spicy flavor.

Clam juice: A commercial shellfish-flavored broth used in soups and sauces. It is low in fat but high in sodium.

Clarified butter: Butter that has been cleared of the dairy solids.

Conch: A large saltwater mollusk, similar to a snail, that lives in the warm waters of the Florida Keys and the Caribbean. The large white foot is edible and the beautiful white-and-pink shell is used for horns and decorations. The conch is a protected species in Florida. Whelk or chopped clams may be substituted in most recipes.

Cream: To blend an ingredient with another to a soft, smooth consistency.

Cream of tartar: A byproduct of wine making, this acidic crystalline substance is used to stabilize beaten egg whites. It also is mixed with baking soda to make baking powder.

Cumin: A spice ground from the dried seeds of the cumin plant. This spice is used extensively in Latin American, Mexican, Indian and North African cooking.

Dijon-style mustard: A prepared mustard flavored with white wine that originated in Dijon, France. Domestic and imported brands are available in grocery stores.

Dredge or dust: To cover or coat food lightly with flour, cornmeal or cracker crumbs.

Drawn butter: Melted butter prepared with flour and water as a sauce.

Evaporated skim milk: Canned skimmed milk that has been reduced by 60 percent in volume through evaporation. Used to add a creamy thickness to soups, sauces and puddings.

Fines herbes: A combination of finely chopped herbs that generally includes chervil, chives, parsley and tarragon. The blend is available in some gourmet stores and supermarkets.

Fish sauce: A thin, salty, dark-brown flavoring agent used in Southeast Asian cooking instead of soy sauce. Called *nam pla* in Thailand and *nuoc nam* in Vietnam, it adds a subtle fish flavor to sauces. Thai brands are less salty.

Fold: A method of combining delicate ingredients such as egg whites or whipped cream, with thicker ingredients. Use a spatula or spoon in a circular motion, cutting through the mixture, scraping along the bottom of the bowl and bringing some of the mixture on the bottom to the top.

Garlic: A member of the lily family that includes onions, leeks, elephant garlic, green onions and shallots. All the members contain a natural chemical called

green onions and shallots. All the members contain a natural chemical called allicin, which may inhibit blood clotting and aid in prevention of coronary heart disease. Garlic may be eaten raw or cooked.

Ginger: An aromatic root of the ginger plant that also includes turmeric and galangal. Fresh ginger adds a spicy hotness to Oriental cooking. Dried ginger is used for baking to make gingersnaps and gingerbread. Preserved or crystallized ginger is used in English cooking to make fruitcakes, puddings and ices.

Hoisin: A sweet-savory paste made from soybeans, garlic, five-spice powder and a small amount of chili. It's used in Chinese, Vietnamese and Thai cooking as a condiment like ketchup, or added to stir-fry dishes, barbecue sauces and dipping sauces.

Julienne: A method of cutting carrots, peppers, jicama, potatoes or other hard vegetables into matchstick slices. Place the vegetable on a board, slice in half lengthwise and into long, thin strips.

Key limes: Small, very tart limes with a yellowish skin that are grown in the Florida Keys, Caribbean and West Indies. They are used to make Key Lime Pie, marinades and sauces.

Long-grain rice: Slender grains, either white, tan or deep brown that cooks into separate, fluffy grains. Long-grain rice is best used in salads, side dishes, pilafs and soup.

Medium-grain rice: This rice is slightly longer than the Oriental short-grain and less sticky. It is best used in Oriental cooking, fried rice, salads, pilafs or jambalaya.

Puree: To chop food so finely in a blender, food processor or food mill that it becomes a smooth, thick sauce. A puree is also a sauce made from pureed vegetables, fruit, seafood or meat.

Reduce: To decrease the volume of a liquid by rapid boiling in an uncovered pan. As the volume decreases, the flavors intensify and the consistency thickens. Reduction sauces can be very flavorful yet lower in fat than sauces made with cream, flour or eggs.

Short-grain rice: Short, chubby grains, either white or brown that sticks together in clumps after cooking, making it easy to eat with chopsticks. Short-grain rice is best used in Oriental dishes such as sushi, rice pancakes and dessert puddings.

Rice vinegar: A mild, white, pleasant-tasting Oriental vinegar made from rice and alcohol. Far less sour than American vinegars, it can be used without oil on salads or cooked vegetables and added to sauces and soups. It is available in Oriental markets and the ethnic foods section of most grocery stores.

Ricotta: A cheese product made from the whey drained from provolone and mozzarella. It is bland and has a soft consistency. Brands made from part-skim milk are low in fat and cholesterol. Used in pasta dishes, dips and desserts.

Roux: A blend of oil or butter and flour used to thicken sauces and gravies. The oil or butter are mixed together over heat and a liquid is whisked in. As the liquid reaches the boiling point it binds with the flour and thickens into a sauce.

Sherry: The English name given to a fortified amber-colored wine named after Jerez, Spain where it was first made. Small amounts of dry sherry add a distinctive flavor and aroma to soups and sauces. Sweet sherry can be used in desserts. It contains no fat and most of the calories evaporate with cooking.

Water bath: The French call this cooking technique bain-marie. It involves placing a container (casserole dish, bowl, pan, etc.) in a large shallow pan of warm water. The bath surrounds the food with gentle heat. Water baths are used to cook delicate dishes such as custards, sauces and savory mousses.

Wild rice: Not a rice but a seed of a native grass plant. Long, dark-brown kernels that take up to 40 minutes to cook. Wild rice has a chewy texture and nutty flavor and it is not sticky. It is best used in salads, pilafs, stuffings, pancakes and side dishes.

Zest: The colored exterior peel of citrus fruits that contains highly flavored oils. Zest is used to add citrus flavor to sauces, cakes, baking and frozen desserts. Orange and lemon zest are the most commonly used in recipes. Avoid using the zest of Key limes, which becomes bitter.

Index